CREATING CHAMPIONS

Canadian Cataloguing in Publication Data
K-Burr, Betska, 1952-
Creating champions

Includes bibliographical references and index.
ISBN 0-7715-9042-3

1. Incentives in industry.   2. Employee motivation.
I. Title

HF5549.5.I5K28 1994   658.3'142   C94-930684-3

Macmillan Canada wishes to thank the Canada Council and the Ontario Ministry of Culture and Communications for supporting its publishing program.

Macmillan Canada
A Division of Canada Publishing Corporation
Toronto, Canada

1 2 3 4 5   98 97 96 95 94

Printed in Canada

To John, lots of "tsoms" for your trust and faith in me,
for your joie de vivre.

To Tania, for loving me as only a child can.

To Bella, I love you Mom.

MONEY-BACK GUARANTEE

The concepts in this book are so sound that I guarantee you or your organization will benefit from the concepts. If after implementing all of the applications in the Model for Creating Champions upon which this book is based, you have not been able to raise the morale of your organization, return the book in good condition along with your receipt to K-Burr & Associates for a full refund.

Betska K-Burr

K-Burr & Associates
P.O. Box 21024
London, Ontario N6J 1G0
Canada

TABLE OF CONTENTS

PART A: CREATING CHAMPIONS

INTRODUCTION — GETTING YOUR PEOPLE FIRED UP TO PRODUCE
                MORE AND BETTER

Your Sales Reps will sell more...your Plant Workers will produce more and better quality products...your people will be more concerned about sales and profits...your Service Techs will provide better technical services...your Managers will learn the tricks of building a team...government employees will improve their service to the taxpayer...employee morale will soar...profits will increase...and you'll have fun!

PART B: WHY AND HOW TO CONDUCT SUCCESSFUL RECOGNITION PROGRAMS

Build a stronger team...improve morale...achieve new sales heights...reduce costs...increase profits...improve cash flow...reduce inventory levels...reduce receivables...improve productivity...sell off used product...improve quality of customer service...get closer to your customer...expedite the learning curve of new products...build awareness of your company...generate free P.R. and advertising...overcome staff uncertainty during mergers/acquisitions...recognize and praise your service heroes or top achievers...have fun.

PART C: 4 MAGICAL ANNUAL RECOGNITION/INCENTIVE PROGRAMS

PART D: 14 TESTED, DYNAMIC, SHORT-TERM RECOGNITION/INCENTIVE PROGRAMS

PART E:

LIST OF CHARTS

ACKNOWLEDGMENTS

As you walk through life there are a few people who leave their mark on your soul.

Mike Pascoe was the type of leader of whom everyone dreams. Mike trusted me to "do my own thing" no matter how wacky the idea! Brenda Hayter and Jill Harness, two of my best buddies, are beacons of joy. Such bonds of friendship help transform all of life's roadblocks into opportunities. And then there's Jane Atkinson, Marketing Director Extraordinaire! Kind, caring, intelligent, enthusiastic and optimistic are all words to describe a Jane who has escalated my career as a professional speaker. John Burr, with his enviable sense of humor and enormous love of family, inspired me to write this book. Without his support, this book would not have come to life. God has blessed me with His love and a host of friends and family who make my life complete.

INTRODUCTION

> **A MASSIVE PARADIGM SHIFT IS OCCURRING WHICH DEMANDS THAT EMPLOYEES BE EMPOWERED TO INNOVATE TO BETTER SERVE THE CUSTOMER**

Dear Readers:

As you proceed through the pages in this book, you'll notice one prevailing thought: A massive paradigm shift is occurring in the way we run our organizations. Those organizations who wish to thrive in a time of rampant change need to inspire their people to be innovative when it comes to serving the customer. Only then can they expect to leave their mark in a highly competitive world. Inspiration through motivation. That's the paradigm shift.

In 1991, a study by Louis Harris showed that 41% of Americans and 39% of Canadians like their jobs. If 60% don't like their jobs, they probably aren't inspired or innovative. We've got a long way to go to raise the morale and productivity of the majority of employees.

Creating Champions needs to be read by both management leaders and non-management leaders. Indeed, everyone in the organization must take on a leadership role when it comes to servicing the customer. As I see it, this is an important element of the paradigm shift. No longer can we afford to have employees who simply "go through the motions" in an eight-hour day. Everyone must be inspired to be creative and innovative to better serve the customer. Everyone is a leader in the role they currently find themselves in.

> **MOTIVATION MEANS CREATING AN ENVIRONMENT IN WHICH PEOPLE CAN GROW**

Managers in both the public and private sectors will benefit from the Model for Creating Champions – the model upon which this book is based. When all ten applications in the model are executed and working, only then will a motivational environment be created. Customers like doing business with positive people. The end result should be increased productivity and happier, more loyal employees and customers. The Model for Creating Champions appears in Figure 1 at the end of this introduction. It includes building a team, developing a mission, recognition and praise, and more.

Non-management readers will already know that it is possible that their management may not know how to create a motivating environment. Take it upon yourself to guide them. As a non-manager, I was continually making suggestions on how to improve the organization. We all have an impact on the future of the organization. Management leaders no longer have the time to be the sole initiators of innovation. Secondly, non-management leaders need to feel needed. By using the brainpower and creativity of <u>everyone</u> in the organization, we'll be far ahead of the competition. Besides, who's closest to the customer?

BARRIERS BETWEEN MANAGEMENT AND STAFF CAN BE BROKEN USING THE YO-YO PRINCIPLE

People at work erect barriers between management and staff. We build walls instead of bridges. The concepts in *Creating Champions,* when implemented, will help your organization overcome communication roadblocks. By encouraging employees and management to communicate openly, challenges can be overcome and opportunities seized. Bottom-up and top-down communication, when conducted openly, is what I call the Yo-Yo Principle. Picture yourself playing with a yo-yo. Apply the right amount of energy and the yo-yo keeps spinning up and down. Take away the energy and the yo-yo spirals out of control. The energy in any organization is communication: poor communication may cause your organization to falter. Apply the ten applications in the Model for Creating Champions and the staff will suddenly love coming to work in the morning. And, customers will like doing business with your company.

Middle managers can just as easily implement the Model as can the Big Cheese. And, no, it doesn't have to start at the top: after all, as a middle manager, your job is to look after your people.

The following story is a classic example of the Yo-Yo Principle. The seed for my motivational program (one of the most effective I've ever encountered) was planted by an accounting clerk.

MANAGERS SHUFFLE PAPER
COACHES INSPIRE PEOPLE

As a national marketing manager, it was my job to keep the salespeople excited about making cold calls. Tough job! Most people hate cold calling with a passion. I designed a business plan which called for monthly, quarterly, and annual incentive programs. One day, as I was walking down the hall at corporate head office, Mike, an accounting clerk, stopped me in my tracks and said, "Good morning Betska, I see you've launched another incentive program for the salespeople." "Yes," I replied with my characteristic enthooosiasm (that's the correct spelling in my book!) "Isn't it exciting!" Mike's response caught me off guard. "Well," he said, "why is it that the salespeople get to have all the fun in this organization?" Back in my office, I determined that what Mike was really saying was: "How come the salespeople get all the recognition and praise around here?" I hastily gathered together my marketing team and designed an inspiring, motivational program for the entire organization, including distributors (see "Undercover Agent" page 183 for the program details).

Thoroughly pleased with the program, I took it to the V.P. for his blessing. He read it and asked, "Why would you want to run such a program?" I explained that some employees felt that senior management believed the salespeople were the most valued in the company. To my dismay, he replied, "Well, aren't they?" He argued that without salespeople there would be no customers and no revenue. What he didn't understand is that all departments are equal in status:

Without manufacturing, there would be no product.

Without administration, orders would not be shipped.

Without technical service, customers could not keep their products in good running order.

Without personnel, employees would not get paid.

Without finance, customers would not be billed.

Sales is only one aspect of a team. If sales is made to feel superior to everyone else how effective would that company be? How much trust would there be between members? How high would be the level of support for each other? How cohesive would they be as a group? How easily could they reach their goals and grow the organization? And, wouldn't customers sense the lack of teamwork?

The moral of the story is this:

BEFORE YOU CAN BUILD AN EFFECTIVE TEAM EVERYONE MUST FEEL EQUALLY IMPORTANT TO THE ORGANIZATION

Start building your team from the top. Human beings are great mimics – if they see an incredible team at the top, chances are the team spirit will filter down through the ranks. Teach people how to be team players: there are numerous excellent organizations around who have the expertise to help you.

When we ran the program we were amazed at the results – it motivated the entire company. The teamwork was awe-inspiring. We should have bottled the excitement and sold it! The effect on the company was everlasting.

Managers shuffle paper. Coaches inspire people. Anybody can shuffle paper. It's a tougher job to be an effective coach and leader who inspires people.

Before we go any further in this introduction, grab a pen or pencil and respond "yes" or "no" to this survey:

1) Do you know your organization's Customer Service   __yes __no
Index? (ie: what your customers think of your service)

2) Do you know your employee satisfaction index?   __yes __no
(ie: what your employees think about your organization)

3) Does each manager receive feedback from their staff   __yes __no
on their strengths and areas of improvement?

4) Does each manager help each employee set their   __yes __no
own written goals and then help them to achieve
those goals?

5) Does your organization have an official Recognition   __yes __no
and Praise Program whereby ALL employees can be
recognized for a job well done?

6) Is your management team practising management by   __yes __no
communication? (Are they communicating well?)

Tally up the number of "yes" check marks. How many of you answered "yes" to all six questions? I speak to and train thousands of people annually. Only a meagre 1 to 2% answer "yes" to all six questions. Why only 1 to 2%? Two reasons: Either they don't believe that this paradigm shift in leadership is critical to growth or they haven't been taught how to be an effective coach and leader for this challenging decade. Inspiration through motivation. That's the ticket.

To those of you who answered "yes" to each question, I stand up and salute you. You are among the few who know that motivation means creating an environment in which people can grow. But don't stop reading now! I guarantee that you'll find at least one gem of an idea in this book which you haven't seen or heard of before. Aside from the charts full of inspiring ideas in the front of the book, there are unique recognition/incentive ideas at the back of the book.

To those of you who couldn't answer "yes" to each question, I hope that you will embrace the concepts presented. You may even find that the changing demands and needs of both your customers and employees require you to change your corporate culture. This is no easy task. Both customer and employee groups are made up of people who have different beliefs, values, cultures, and needs. We are living in an age of communication. Nobody wants to be treated like a mushroom anymore. We must change our management style to keep up with the changing needs of employees and customers. Are you up to the challenge?

> **CHANGE IS CRITICAL TO GROWTH BUT YOUR PERSONAL PROGRESS IS OPTIONAL**

If we agree that changing our management style is critical to growth, action is required. If we agree that, as non-managers, we must consider changing our communication style with our customers, then read on. Change will continue to happen. We are operating in what social commentators are already calling the most turbulent decade in history. The early 21st century won't be much different. You can learn to change in order to create a motivating environment in which people can grow or you can get left behind. Change is critical to growth, but your personal progress is optional.

> **BY INCREASING MORALE BY JUST 15%, YOU MAY INCREASE PRODUCTIVITY UP TO 40%**

Research says that if you increase morale by just 15%, you may increase productivity up to 40%. Think about the effect on the bottom line! For those of you in the public sector, think of what that increase in productivity can do for you. Reduce costs perhaps? Generate innovative ideas for servicing the customer? The benefits are endless.

Creating Champions is divided up into two main sections. In the first section, a chapter is devoted to each application in the Model. This Model turns managers into coaches and leaders. It creates champions who will be inspired to deliver legendary customer service. The second section in the book is devoted to recognition/incentive programs.

RECOGNITION AND INCENTIVE PROGRAMS ARE MASTERFUL PERFORMANCE BUILDERS

There is a misconception about incentive or recognition programs that must be dispelled. Incentive and recognition programs are *not* just for salespeople. *All* employees in both the pubic and private sectors will flourish under these programs.

The following examples provided to me by R & D Corporate Services (Mississauga, Ontario) clearly point out the power of recognition programs. Companies like R & D are invaluable in custom-designing the right kinds of gifts for recognition programs. In this first example, note the emphasis on "exceeding" customer expectations.

The Ontario Business Sales and Service (Operations) division of Bell has a "Quality in Action" program that recognizes achievement that "clearly exceeds the expectations as defined by the customer, employees and shareholders." Since its implementation two years ago, many recipients have expressed their pride and appreciation in being nominated and selected for this award. The success of the program and its effect on employees was demonstrated by comments from a manager with over 35 years service. He said that receiving this recognition from his peers meant more to him than to have received Bell's monetary performance award.

The Xerox Canada human resources department was faced with an increasing work load, shrinking staff and a continued desire to provide the most effective long-service recognition to employees. What developed was a congratulatory card with an order form and colour photograph of the gift choices for 20, 25 and 30 years' service. The personal touch renewed enthusiasm in their awards program and delivered a message to employees that they are a special part of the Xerox organization. The administration of the program was taken over by the supplier, R & D Corporate Services, and this enabled Xerox to continue to provide meaningful recognition without burdening the human resources department.

Creating Champions comes complete with dozens of short- and long-term annual recognition/incentive programs. There are programs to improve productivity, reduce costs, build teamwork, increase sales and profits, build awareness, recognize and praise top achievers, reduce receivables, improve service quality, improve product quality, improve dealer relations, boost morale, expedite the learning of new products, overcome staff uncertainty during mergers/acquisitions, and have fun!

All salespeople should check out the incentives section. Use incentives to communicate with your customers – use them to increase your sales per customer and to entice customers back into the fold.

My last introductory words are these: I believe that communication is our biggest challenge. The new leadership paradigm asks you to communicate like you've never communicated before. Application #5 (see "Listen to Your People," page 37) is invaluable for those who need some guidance communicating. Try some of the ideas and follow the Yo-Yo Principle (bottom-up and top-to-bottom communication) to break down those invisible barriers that inherent between management and staff.

THE YO-YO PRINCIPLE ENCOURAGES BOTTOM-UP AND TOP-DOWN COMMUNICATION, BUT IT TAKES GUTS TO FOLLOW IT

Enjoy the read *and* the Incentive Programs – determine which ones you can use to recognize and praise the hard-working employees in your workplace. When your staff succeeds, so do you!

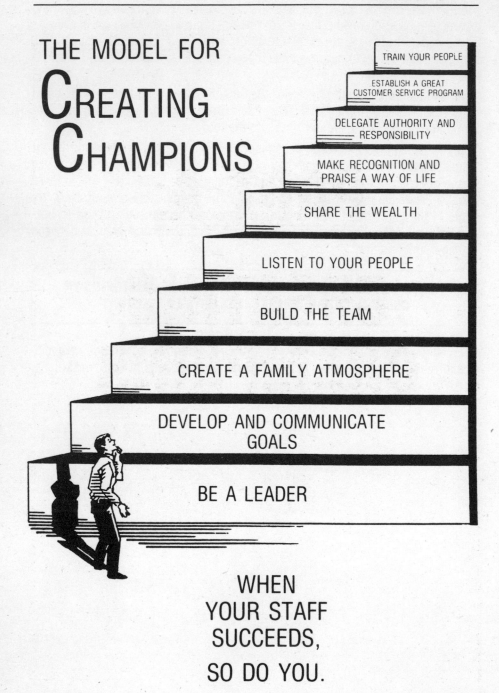

Figure 1 THE MODEL FOR CREATING CHAMPIONS

PART A:

CREATING CHAMPIONS

CREATING CHAMPIONS

> "There are two things people want more than sex and money...recognition and praise."
>
> — Mary Kay Ash

The founder of Mary Kay Cosmetics has unearthed the key to growing a company from an idea to a multi-million dollar empire in a few short years. Lead your people to be successful and they, in turn, will make you successful. Recognize their achievements and praise them for their efforts.

The philosophies of Mary Kay Ash are as old as time. She understands the basic needs of the average worker, "...make people who work for you feel important. If you honor and serve them, they'll honor and serve you."

In Search of Excellence, the book that has revolutionized our thoughts on doing business, studies the management skills of excellent companies. Co-authors Peters and Waterman comment on the wisdom of well-run organizations, "The lesson that the excellent companies have to teach is that... most of their people are made to feel that they are winners.".

Zig Ziglar in his book, *Top Performance*, writes that the foundation for developing yourself and others is wrapped up in this principle: "You can have everything in life you want if you just help enough other people get what they want."

All of these management gurus understand that real managers get things done through people. They know the power of building a highly motivated team capable of achieving results beyond your wildest dreams.

What position of authority do you hold right now? Are you a middle manager of people in your organization? Are you a government manager? Are you a church leader? Do you coach sports? Are you a marketer looking for ways to strengthen your Dealer network? Or, are you the President and CEO of either a small company or an international conglomerate? Whoever you are, wherever you are located, take the next few pages and digest them well. Take these principles and weave them into the fibre of your organization. *Create champions around you and the rewards will appear on the bottom line.*

YOUR PASSPORT TO THE 21st CENTURY

Chart #1, your "PASSPORT TO THE 21st CENTURY" is a powerfully simple passport to financial success. It will carry you well into the next century. Take a moment to think about the four components to the formula. All the best products and services in the world are not going to get you anywhere without a motivated team of champions driving your goals to growth and profitability.

BUSINESS IS:	95% PEOPLE
	5% EVERYTHING ELSE

What happens if the "people" in the name of employees, dealers and customers aren't happy? What if your employees come to work only to collect a pay cheque - they really don't enjoy their jobs. What if your dealers aren't loyal to your company's products and services? What if your customers aren't coming back because they haven't been receiving the service that they were promised? It won't be long before your business is no more. *People drive your business.*

GOVERNMENT

For those government managers who are wondering at the continual reference to "Business", there is an assumption here that each public sector organization is being run as a business. You have revenues from the taxpayer's pocket and you have expenses. Most of you will strive to balance your budgets while others are profit centres. Your "Product" is your customer service to the taxpayers who are paying for that service.

PASSPORT TO THE 21st CENTURY

CREATE CHAMPIONS OF SATISFIED AND MOTIVATED EMPLOYEES.

PLUS

DEVELOP A CUSTOMER SERVICE PROGRAM WHICH WILL KEEP YOUR CUSTOMERS LOYAL AND IN THE FOLD.

PLUS

OFFER WORLD-CLASS QUALITY PRODUCTS AND SERVICES. DIFFERENTIATE YOURSELF FROM THE COMPETITION.

PLUS

ENERGIZE YOUR TEAM OF CHAMPIONS TO WORK TOWARDS A COMMON GOAL OF COMPANY GROWTH AND PROFITS.

THE RESULT:

FINANCIAL SUCCESS WELL INTO THE 21st CENTURY

Chart #1

In a recent conversation with a union leader from a federal government department, I was once again reminded that government employees are perhaps the least motivated of all employees. In reality, they should be the most motivated. They are almost guaranteed a life-time position - taxpayers have refillable pockets.

So what is the problem? The "Passport to the 21st Century" carries the answer. Motivated employees, with a strong customer service program, all working towards common goals, will result in an energized government organization and a much happier taxpayer.

DEALERS

Throughout this book you will find reference to "Dealers". By Dealers, I mean any type of distributor of your product that you use to get your product to market. Dealers present an interesting opportunity to you as a leader of your organization. They are independently owned and operated companies upon whom you rely to do a good selling job to move your product. A Dealer is both a customer of yours and an employee. The Dealers must be made to feel a part of your team. When you create champions of them and of their employees and make them all feel like winners, your Dealers will reward you with loyalty. This loyalty will translate itself into continued growth and profits.

"Star Reach - A Dealer Program", in Part C of this book, is specifically designed for assisting you in fostering loyalty from your Dealers.

CREATING CHAMPIONS
— TEN APPLICATIONS —

> **A SATISFIED, MOTIVATED TEAM OF EMPLOYEES OR DEALERS ALL WORKING TOWARDS A COMMON GOAL OF COMPANY GROWTH AND PROFITS WILL ENERGIZE YOUR ORGANIZATION FOR FINANCIAL SUCCESS IN THE 90's AND BEYOND.**

Take a moment to read through the ten applications for Creating Champions in Chart #2.

Did you buy all 10 applications? Are you wondering what on earth these 10 applications have to do with motivating employees? The old theory of injecting

CREATING CHAMPIONS

WHEN YOUR STAFF SUCCEEDS, SO DO YOU.

— TEN APPLICATIONS —

1. **BE A LEADER** - The Power of Example

2. **DEVELOP AND COMMUNICATE GOALS** - Everyone Must Be Rowing In The Same Boat

3. **CREATE A FAMILY ATMOSPHERE** - Have Fun

4. **BUILD THE TEAM** - Challenge Them To Build A Future

5. **LISTEN TO YOUR PEOPLE** - Can You *Hear* What They're Saying?

6. **SHARE THE WEALTH** - Hinge Compensation to Performance

7. **MAKE RECOGNITION AND PRAISE A WAY OF LIFE** - Be Proud of Their Efforts

8. **DELEGATE AUTHORITY AND RESPONSIBILITY** - Trust Your People

9. **TRAIN YOUR PEOPLE** - Invest In Your Future

10. **ESTABLISH A GREAT CUSTOMER SERVICE PROGRAM** - Your backbone for the 90's and into the 21st century

Chart #2

a quick-fix incentive program to motivate employees has gone the way of the brontosaurus. *To motivate employees for the long term, you must change your corporate culture.*

In addition, the quickie programs can often backfire if the troops are generally unhappy. Here are two very recent examples which were related to me by unhappy employees.

CASE #1

A government department devised a contest to develop a logo for a specific health program. All employees were given the opportunity to design a logo. The designer of the chosen logo would win a prize. More importantly, the new design would become the logo for the program. In the end, the designer got her prize but the logo was trashed. No one knows why. A new logo, ostensibly designed by an ad agency, now graces the literature of the health program.

How do you think this employee feels after having been promised a place of glory? The winner was never told why her logo was not used. The questions we need to ask are:

1) Why was the winning logo not used?

2) Why was the change in recognition not communicated to the employee?

3) Is this an example of good leadership style?

4) What impact would this situation have on team building?

5) Would you say that there is a family atmosphere in this organization?

6) Are they listening to their people but not hearing what they're saying?

7) Do you think the employees will get excited the next time an incentive program is launched?

8) As a manager, your employees are your customers. Was this customer well treated?

9) What effect do you think this faux pas will have on the way this employee treats the taxpayer?

Case #1 is a classic example of how incentive programs can bomb if the organization is run ineffectively. Here's the first lesson:

INCENTIVE PROGRAMS CAN ASSIST YOU IN TEMPORARILY BOOSTING MORALE. TO HAVE AN ENDURING EFFECT, TREAT YOUR EMPLOYEES WELL ON A DAILY BASIS BY RUNNING YOUR ORGANIZATION WITH FEELING. WHEN YOUR STAFF SUCCEEDS, SO DO YOU.

Chart #2 is the way that organizations can put "feeling" back into their corporate culture. It *can and will* pay off.

CASE #2

A manufacturing company was having difficulty with employees who were coming in late and leaving early. The employees were on a flex-time program which allowed them to come in anytime between 8 a.m. and 10 a.m. just as long as they put in an 8 hour day. With several employees per manager, it was difficult to keep track of everyone's hours.

In order to correct the problem, management implemented an incentive program. All employees who put in a full 8 hour day for one month straight would receive a T-shirt.

There are several questions in this example that we need to ask:
1) Is the company communicating well with its people? Do the employees know what is expected of them?
2) Are the Leader Managers in the company setting an example?
3) Are their employees happy? Or, are they late because they hate their jobs?
4) Is management listening to its people?
5) Is the T-shirt program the way to fix the problem?
6) Is this good use of a recognition and praise program?
7) How is the customer being serviced if the employees arrive late and leave early?

Here's the second lesson:

EXPECT THE BEST FROM YOUR PEOPLE. COMMUNICATE YOUR EXPECTATIONS. CONSCIOUSLY WORK AT IDENTIFYING AND ACKNOWLEDGING GOOD BEHAVIOUR. FOR PERSONNEL ISSUES, USE INCENTIVE PROGRAMS TO REWARD SOLID SOLUTIONS INSTEAD OF QUICK FIXES. WHEN YOUR STAFF SUCCEEDS, SO DO YOU.

This company should start at the beginning again and ask themselves why they don't have champions working for them. By making the ten applications of Creating Champions work, the lateness and absenteeism should diminish.

Creating champions is tough work. It may mean changing your corporate culture, your organizational structure and the way you do business with your customer.

To be financially successful moving into the 21st century, act now. The children of the baby boomers are children who are being raised in an age of openness, communication and feeling. They have high expectations. They are demanding. In addition to this, they are and will be your employees and customers for a long time.

Now, go back and reread Creating Champions - Chart #2. This is what your organization needs to do to keep your employees satisfied and motivated in the 90's and beyond.

Each application in Chart #2 is dealt with in some detail within its own chapter. There are several basic themes running through the chapters: make your people feel important, recognize and praise their efforts and when they succeed, so will you.

BE A LEADER - THE POWER OF EXAMPLE

> "The mechanics of running a business are really not very complicated when you get down to essentials. You have to make some stuff and sell it to somebody for more than it cost you. That's about all there is to it, except for a few million details."
>
> — John L. McCaffrey

How true it is! I've searched the learned halls of libraries and the depths of my brain for a good, short definition of leadership. I came to one conclusion. It's impossible to define leadership in any short, concise way. It's too complex.

A Leader can be a supervisor or department manager, business owner or corporate C.E.O. The term "Leader" applies to anyone who manages people, directly or indirectly. A Leader is the person who guides his/her people to be successful. He/she will take all ten of the applications in Chart #2 very seriously. A Leader knows that by creating champions of people, he/she will also succeed. A Leader is an enthusiast, a coach, a facilitator, a builder, a cheerleader, and a nurturer of champions. A Leader exhibits passion, sensitivity, consistency, caring, attention to detail and knows the influence of drama. A Leader is a good administrator, a manager of paper and people, a motivator, a planner, a trainer, a problem solver, a psychologist and, last but not least, a guardian of the bottom line.

Does this person sound like God? A successful Leader must be strong and talented. Does he or she have to be good at everything? No. But good leaders know that by setting an example, by exhibiting excellent people skills and by hiring the right people, chances are your organization will run smoothly. A Leader doesn't have to know how the equipment runs in the plant or the intricate details on writing a computer program: you hire good people to perform those functions. Leaders must know, however, how to manage their employees to become champions at their jobs.

> ## IT'S NOT THE WORK THAT KEEPS PEOPLE IN THE JOB, IT'S THE BOSS, IT'S THE PEOPLE

The champion leadership style that you exhibit will be transmitted to your employees, your suppliers, your customers and your dealers. For example, the attitude of a Leader will filter down through all the layers and become a part of the corporate culture. If you're an enthusiast who truly cares about your people and your customers, your entire organization will demonstrate that same attitude towards each other and towards your customers, suppliers and dealers.

Here's a gem I came across recently: "When they say a man is a 'born executive' they mean his father owns the business!" No one is born a Leader. It takes desire, training, experience, sensitivity and more sensitivity. Long gone is the attitude of the 1960s. Management by fear simply doesn't work in today's world. Management by caring will take you into the 21st century.

Take a second now to read Chart #3, entitled "Job Description of a Leader." A Leader is 12 people in one. No wonder it's a tough job! The next few pages explain the role of the Leader who wears each one of the hats listed in the Job Description.

ADMINISTRATOR

A Leader has to be good at shuffling paper, each page no more than twice. Not once. Not three times. Twice. Once to read and once to follow-up, if required. The majority of your paper flow can be read once and filed. For action-oriented paper, delegate most of it and have a good follow-up system set up by your assistant. A trained assistant won't necessarily pass the paper back to you. He or she will simply inform you that the task was done, or remind you that a project is due. Recycling paper does not mean seeing it again!

JOB DESCRIPTION
OF
A LEADER

AN ADMINISTRATOR

A MARKETER

A MANAGER

A SALESPERSON

A MOTIVATOR

A BUILDER

A TRAINER

A FACILITATOR

A PROBLEM-SOLVER

A PLANNER

A PSYCHOLOGIST

A GUARDIAN OF THE BOTTOM LINE

AN INNOVATOR

CHART #3

Spend as little time as possible shuffling paper. You are needed to help make decisions in meetings and to walk around the office to keep on top of the day-to-day running of your organization. You need to make field visits and keep close to the customer.

MARKETER

A Leader needs to know the business. He or she has to understand the market place, the competition, the customers and the product. Knowing how to make the customer buy is all-important. We've all come across companies who have felt confident about their markets — until they had some market research done. Don't become complacent: it's easy to lose touch. Work in the field. Visit customers. Keep on top of the competition. Be creative, in terms of communicating the strengths of your company's products and services. Don't forget the services. Organizations must be service-oriented if they are to be on the leading edge in the '90s and beyond. Remember to differentiate yourself from the competition.

MANAGER

A Leader is a manager of people and time — a mover and a shaker! He or she is acutely aware of all the projects and tasks that need to be done. Do you own a good time-management system? If not, invest in one. The best system works on an 8 1/2 x 11 inch paper system because much of the world operates on that size of paper. Your system should contain the following:

— Daily record of appointments *and* projects.
— Month at a glance.
— Year at a glance.
— A page for listing recurring tasks and events.
— A section to list and keep track of projects that need to be done. This section will identify who the project leader is, the target date and costs where applicable.
— A followup section to ensure that you are on track to meet the organization's goals. You need to be constantly reminded of your goals.
— A section on hot prospects and warm prospects.
— A section for expenses. Keep your expenses in a pocket for future tallying.
— An A-Z tabbed file for listing the names and phone numbers of accountants, lawyers, friends, relatives, suppliers, dealers, etc. Behind each tab, keep the correspondence that you need to use when you see them next as well as pertinent info about these people.

This system sounds thick in size doesn't it? Well, it need not be. As you can see, your people and time management system will keep you abreast of the important things that are happening or that need to be done. Moreover, it will keep your paper to a minimum and put you out where you belong - with your people, your dealers and your customers.

SALES PERSON

A Leader needs to be a sales person. For example, the 10 applications to Creating Champions must be sold to the managers of your organization. After all, they are the ones who will sell it to their people and make it work. At the same time, you need to sell your ideas upwards to the people to whom you report. Unless, of course, you're in the lucky position of reporting only to yourself!

MOTIVATOR

A Leader is a motivator. Attitudes from above affect the entire organization. In Chart #4, "The Many Facets of a Leader", read through the box entitled "Interpersonal Skills". Yes, a Leader makes the coffee! Are you easy to talk to? Do you know all the names of the people in your organization? It gets a little tough when you hit the 1000th employee but I've seen people do it! John Myser, former President of 3M Canada Inc., had an enormous capacity for names. During his reign, 3M Canada had over 2,000 employees. Yet, you could hear him calling people by name as he walked the halls of the corporate head office.

John Myser was also a Motivator Par Excellence. I will never forget the wisdom of this great man. He implemented "lunch meets" at 3M to which employees would bring their lunch and listen to a topic for an hour. There was a series of lunch meets. At some, he would talk about performance and how no one should be afraid to fail.

> **"FAILURE IS SUCCESS IF WE LEARN FROM IT."**
> **— Malcolm S. Forbes**

On other occasions, John would inform everyone of our company's goals and how all of us were rowing in the same boat. To succeed we must all be riding in the same boat in the right direction - heading for the company's goals.

THE MANY FACETS OF A LEADER

INTERPERSONAL SKILLS

- is an enthusiast
- is a team builder
- is a good listener
- is usually available
- regularly recognizes and praises good work
- gives credit to others
- delegates well and empowers
- promotes from within
- often takes the blame
- prefers eye-to-eye contact versus memos
- communicates goals to everyone in the company
- knows people by name
- supports the ideas of others
- makes things look easy
- works hard but has a balanced life
- makes coffee
- expects the best
- challenges people
- is easy to talk to
- inspires loyalty
- inspires ideas/suggestions/innovation
- makes everyone feel important
- enjoys the jobs, has fun
- sets a good example
- is a visionary
- is a risk-taker
- is a quality master

MAJOR ASSETS

- intelligent
- competent
- passionate
- caring
- sensitive
- consistent
- tough
- trusting
- humble
- fair
- decisive
- persistent
- honest
- respectful
- tolerant
- objective
- open-minded
- committed
- approachable
- flexible

Chart #4

And then there were lunch meets where musicians, the local heart transplant team, ministers, etc. were invited in to give us "A Whack on the Side of the Head," (also the name of a book by Roger von Oech). Myser's philosophy is one in which I also firmly believe. Expose your employees to a myriad of different ideas and philosophies by taking their minds outside of the workplace and they will repay you by being more creative on the inside.

Remember that there are employees who work and then go straight home. They lead very sheltered lives with little exposure to the outside world. Help them to enrich their lives.

A good Motivator exhibits all the points listed in the "Interpersonal Skills" column of Chart #4. He/she also carries all the assets listed in the "assets" column of Chart #4.

Wise Leaders treat their employees like family. They teach them, motivate them, support them and reward them. On average, an employee spends 70% of his/her wakeful hours either at work, getting ready for work or commuting to the office. There's no doubt about it. When you dedicate that much time to your job, you *are* family!.

In short, a Leader is a Motivator by example, a Motivator by caring. Treat your people well, care for them and they will reward you with success.

BUILDER

A Leader is a builder. With the strength of a motivated staff, you will build the organization that you want. Together you are building the "House of Co. A".

TRAINER

A Leader is a trainer. Ken Blanchard and Spencer Johnson in *The One Minute Manager* are brilliant in their observation of people. "Everyone is a potential winner. Some people are disguised as losers, don't let their appearances fool you." It is usually the gregarious employees who get all the attention and who seem the brightest. The quiet, silent one in the corner may be your brightest star. Einstein was a classic example. Give all of your people the opportunity to learn. Some will need encouragement, others will take anything they can get.

Fast forward to Application #9 for more valuable information on Training Your People. (But don't forget to come back here to finish this section!)

FACILITATOR

As a facilitator, a Leader makes things happen by tracking the progress of the organization in meeting its goals. Keep everyone on track. Help those who aren't on track. Make the goals appear simple by guiding your people to achieve their goals.

PROBLEM SOLVER

As managers of people, we are constantly solving problems. A Leader's role as a problem solver is to ensure that your people feel comfortable enough to approach you about a problem. When was the last time one of your employees came in to talk to you about a problem? People generally don't have difficulty discussing technical problems with their superiors. If the problem is a feelings-related one, people tend to bottle things up inside. Maybe they're not getting along with a peer. Maybe they're not getting along with a customer. Build your reputation as someone to whom they can come to help solve all their work-related problems. Build a feeling of trust between you and each employee. You will be rewarded with a loyal and content staff.

PLANNER

A Leader is a planner - a Strategic Planner. Somehow the word "Strategic" has never sat well within the neurons of my brain. It seems to scare the h--- out of people. It's easier to think in terms of this - a Leader must plan to shape the future of the organization. John Naisbitt, author of the nationwide #1 best-seller *Megatrends*, writes of the megatrends that are defining a new society, a new world. It's crucial for America to change the way we plan. The average Strategic Plan for the Japanese spans 22 years. In America, we think short-term goals and short-term profits. Writes Naisbitt, "The most reliable way to anticipate the future is by understanding the present.".

For further insight on how to develop goals, fast forward to Application #2 of this book.

PSYCHOLOGIST

A Leader must know what makes people tick. Which are the buttons to push? Where is the Achilles' heel? A psychologist listens exceptionally well and asks a lot of questions. He or she lets the employee come up with the answers unless there is a stumbling block. At that time, personal guidance and direction are in order. A Leader corrects performance in private and always gives at least a second chance. Be open and honest with your people and they'll return the favor. A Leader is a stabilizing influence in any crisis and should be, at turns, tough and gentle.

GUARDIAN OF THE BOTTOM LINE

Someone once said that Hard work is the yeast that raises the dough. No doubt about it: it takes hard work and good leadership to bring in the sheaves of wheat. And, it takes even more work to keep costs down. There is no magic to guarding the bottom line:

UNDERSTAND WHAT BUSINESS RATIOS AND REPORTS YOU NEED TO MONITOR. FOLLOW THE PROGRESS MONTHLY. MAKE SURE YOU'RE MEETING YOUR REVENUE AND COST GOALS. IF NOT, FIND OUT WHY AND FIX IT.

Leaders, however, know that if they are applying all ten applications of *Creating Champions* Chart #2, the bottom line usually looks after itself.

INNOVATOR

Picture if you will an automobile with two wheels — a front and back wheel. This vehicle is called the Vehicle for Progress because it depicts the six vision skills we must embrace if we are to successfully move into the 21st century.

The front-wheel skills are *leadership, teamwork* and *aligned empowerment.* Aligned empowerment simply means that each employee is empowered to make decisions just as long as those decisions are aligned with the mission, vision and goals of the organization. These front-wheel skills *steer* the organization in the direction of the six vision skills. They are the easiest to master.

The leadership paradigm shift adds a back wheel to our vehicle. It is the back-wheel skills that often present the greatest challenge. These three vision skills are *risk, innovation* and *change management.* While the front-wheel skills steer the organization, the back-wheel skills *propel* the organization forward. By taking risks and being innovative, only then can we progress. Because employees often have difficulty making that quantum leap to being innovative about how to serve the customer, it is important that they are challenged to be creative.

The glue that holds your organization together is trust and communication. If trust exists between management and staff, employees feel more secure in suggesting ideas for improvement. Open communication ensures that everyone understands what is expected of them as your organization moves forward.

DEVELOP AND COMMUNICATE GOALS - EVERYONE MUST BE ROWING IN THE SAME BOAT

> "**A** man without a purpose is like a ship without a rudder."
> — Thomas Carlyle

There is no analogy more powerful. A ship without a rudder would be lost forever. An organization without a set of goals has no purpose, no direction. As the old saying goes, *how can you get anywhere if you don't know where you're going?*

Some people call these goals business planning. Others get a little fancier and call it strategic planning. I simply call it "Planning to Shape Your Future". As I mentioned earlier, one of the major reasons why the Japanese have been so successful is the fact that they are experts at planning. And, at sticking to their plans. The average Japanese business plan is 22 years. How long is yours? In North America we tend to think short-term revenue and short-term profits. That's fine if you want to sell your company in 3 years time. If you want to be a major player in the market place, you must invest in your future. The car industry is still the best classic example of Japanese planning prowess. We remember it well - so do the American car manufacturers!. The plan called for marketing a so-so quality car at unheard of prices. They bought market share. As the years progressed, the Japanese produced better and better products. Today, their top-of-the-line models compete head-to-head on quality with the best of North American, British and German models. And what happened to their pricing? With consumer confidence high, they can now command higher prices. You can bet that their bottom line looks terrific as well. Oh, I realize that there are other parts to this story such as the Deming principle, and knowing what the customer wanted (small versus large cars); however, they were all part of the master plan.

OUR CHANGING WORLD

Modern technology has accelerated changes in the market place. Demographic and lifestyle changes have delivered a heavy blow to mass marketing and brand loyalty. Political eruptions in the Middle East have changed our thinking patterns. Businesses are casting an eager eye to the eastern block countries now that the Berlin Wall is relegated to the history books. Hong Kong will soon move from a capitalist to a communist environment when the Chinese take over in 1997.

''Deregulation has splintered the financial, travel and communications sectors into a shoppers paradise of choices,'' say Rapp and Collins in their book *Maximarketing*. Computers, 1-800#'s, coupons, sampling, credit cards, satellites, and shopping from your television set have all changed the way we buy.

There is a new playing field out there and it changes rapidly. So, how can you plan if changes are rampant and unpredictable?

> **"THE GREAT SUCCESSFUL MEN OF THE WORLD HAVE USED THEIR IMAGINATION...THEY THINK AHEAD AND CREATE THEIR MENTAL PICTURE, AND THEN GO TO WORK MATERIALIZING THAT PICTURE IN ALL ITS DETAILS, FILLING IN HERE, ADDING A LITTLE THERE, ALTERING THIS A BIT AND THAT A BIT, BUT STEADILY BUILDING - STEADILY BUILDING."**
> **— Robert Collier**

Just as Collier states, you draw the plan and frequently have to make adjustments to account for demographic and lifestyle changes.

THE PLANNING PROCESS

Keep the process simple. That I've learned from experience. People are so busy with their daily work that they hate to take time out to plan. Yet, it's the most important part of keeping a business alive and prospering. If you keep it simple, everyone will be happy with the process. Conduct the planning process off-site; a resort will stimulate the creative juices. Two to three days should get you there.

> **EVERYONE IN THE ORGANIZATON MUST BE COMMITTED TO REACHING THE SAME GOALS.**

Your planning team should consist of about 15 people made up of senior and middle management- your brightest and most creative people. Combine age groups and sex as well. Sound like a lot of people? Not when you want to do some serious planning. Besides, during the process, you don't have the 15 people in one room for very long. They will be split up into 5 groups of 3 for the workshops. It's a good idea to have a professional strategic planner working with you just to keep you on track.

Chart #5, "Shaping Your Future", summarizes the 7 quick planning steps to follow. The ensuing pages provide the detail for each step. Quick and easy.

Quick steps 1, 2 and 3 can be collected by the Leader prior to the meeting. I firmly believe that the President/CEO must be the Leader of "Shaping Your Future". He/she must buy into the Plan and sell down.

The Leader should give some thought to Quick Step #4 before the meeting. What is your vision for the company? Where do you want it to go? The workshop teams need to have a rough idea of your goals and be in agreement with them. From this point, they can set objectives and plans for their own departments. For example, by knowing what the company's sales goals are for the next 20 years, they'll be able to plan staffing, products, markets, training, etc.

The meeting agenda for "Shaping Your Future" should look something like this:

DAY ONE

The Leader reviews Quick Steps 1, 2, and 3 to get everyone thinking along the same vein. Arrive at consensus.

Break the participants up into the 5 workshop groups listed in the details for

Quick Step #4. Assign a Leader to each group who has a reputation for getting results. Have them brainstorm on the topics given along with anything else they think is relevant. It'll be interesting to see how their visions compare with yours. They must come back with specific goals for the next 3-20 years.

Reassemble to a full session format and review the results from the 5 groups. Arrive at consensus.

DAY TWO
Break into the 5 teams again and do the detail planning on how they are going to achieve the goals they set in Day One.

DAY THREE
Review all the objectives and plans. Reach consensus.

PLANNING TO SHAPE YOUR FUTURE
— THE PROCESS —

1. DEVELOP A MISSION STATEMENT
- The mission identifies the underlying design, aim or thrust of your organization. It defines the business that you're in.
- What is your product? What markets are you targeting?
- The mission determines the competitive arena in which your organization operates. It defines your distribution network.
- It states how resources will be allocated to different demands, ie; R & D.
- It states the current size of the organization.
- The mission states where you want to be in 5, 10, 15 and 20 years in terms of growth, profits, status, market share, etc.
- The mission should define the operating philosophy of the organization: ethics, pricing, quality, quantity, customer service, market share, ROI-profit, opportunities for employees, role in the markeplace (leader, follower, innovator), etc.

Every employee should be able to read the Mission and understand your organization's goals. They *must* buy into the Mission (you have to sell it) and make it happen.

SHAPING YOUR FUTURE

— 7 QUICK PLANNING STEPS —

1. Develop A Mission Statement, A Vision.

2. Do A Quick Review of the Past and Present.

3. Think About Future Changes to the Business.

4. Where/What Do You Want To Be In One Year? 3 Years?
   Up To 20 Years?

5. Draft The Plans To Help You Get There.

6. Sell The Plan - To Middle & Field Management
                 - To All Employees.

7. Check Your Progress.

Chart #5

PEOPLE MAKE PLANS WORK.
PLANS ALONE SELDOM MAKE PEOPLE WORK.

---

2. DO A QUICK REVIEW OF THE PAST AND PRESENT

- This situational analysis will tell you where you've come from and where you are now.

(a) External Analysis

Currently, what is happening outside that is affecting your business? Factors to look at: political, economic, social, demographic, technological, lifestyle and competitive trends. Threats and opportunities from these trends.

(b) Internal Analysis

Study trends in sales, profits and all relevant business ratios (Debt of equity, ROIC, etc.).

Study your customer base. How fast is it growing?

Are you keeping your customers?

Study the people that work with you. Are they happy?

Look at company ethics, pricing, product quality, manufacturing, customer service, market share, opportunities for personal growth of your employees, training and your role in the market place.

3. THINK ABOUT FUTURE CHANGES TO THE BUSINESS

What will likely be the situation 5-20 years hence from a political, economic, social, demographic, technological, lifestyle and competitive point of view. Use your imagination, gut instincts and sources such as economists, banks and soothsayers to forecast assumptions.

4. WHERE/WHAT DO YOU WANT TO BE IN 3 YEARS? 20 YEARS?

Where do you want the organization to be in 3 years, 5 years, 10 years, 15 years and 20 years.

The objectives for as far out in time as you can go must be "S.M.A.R.T." goals - Specific, Measureable, Attainable, Realistic and Time-Based. Here are some of the factors to look at:

Manufacturing
- Quality
- Quantity
- Labour
- Raw Materials
- Plant Space
- R & D

Sales and Marketing
- Sales Forecasts
- Target Markets
- Market Share
- Products
- Distribution
- Communications
  (Advertising, P.R., Sales Promo,
  Incentive Programs)

Administration
- Inventory
- Warehousing
- Customer Service
- Customs
- Transportation
- Information Databases

Finance
- Profits
- Financial Reports
- Business Ratios
- Money Products
  (ie leasing)
- Cash Flow
- Mergers & Acquisitions

The Leader and Human Resources
- Building a Team
- Creating a Family
- Compensation
- Organizational Structure
- Job Sharing
- Appraisal Program
- Training
- Daycare
- Communications with the Employees
- Recognition and Praise Programs
- Measurement of the Progress of your Business Plans

Draft goals for each area above in detail for 3 years. For example, you will want to know what your sales, profit and business ratio goals are for 3 years out. If you can, do the detail of all the factors for 5 years out. For the remaining 15 years, it may be difficult to attach exact numbers to your plans although it can be done. Whatever you do, though, set a goal. In 5 years, you may wish to be number 4 in the market place with 10% market share. In 15 years, you may wish to be number 2 with 20% market share.

5. DRAFT THE PLANS TO HELP YOU GET THERE

This is the fun part. Put your creative hats on - fire up the right side of your brain. Come up with ways in which you can meet your goals. For example, in order to achieve 25% market share in 5 years, you may have to implement loss leader pricing. Or, you may choose to make your product a household name through extensive advertising. The Canon and Xerox corporations have done this most effectively in the office products business.

For every objective, there must be a plan. From each group assign one person responsible for obtaining results from these plans. They will be the drivers to completing the plan. The best people might be the group Leaders you chose for the workshops.

6. SELL THE PLAN

(a) You will need feedback on the plan from middle managers and field managers. Your most important job is to *sell them* on the vision. They will then be committed to helping the organization achieve the vision.

(b) The *entire company* must be told about the plans to shape your company's future. Have a special fun day set aside at head office and in the field. On that day, order in a cake with a big #'s goal written in icing. Now that you've put your money where your mouth is (no pun intended!), sell your employees on the goals. Tell them how important they are to the vision. Share the Mission Statement with them. Don't let them leave the room until you have a feeling of commitment from them. Answer any questions they may have. Consider their suggestions.

7. CHECK YOUR PROGRESS

All disciplined managers already check the financial numbers on a regular basis. On a semi-annual basis, take a closer look at your objectives and plans. How close are you to meeting your goals? You may have to be ''adding a little there, altering this a bit and that a bit... ''. All the while, though, you are steadily building.

Whatever you do, don't put the plan on a shelf. At your quarterly management meetings (top and middle), bring out your goal sheet and review how you're going to attain those goals.

DON'T LOSE SIGHT OF YOUR GOALS. REVIEW THEM QUARTERLY. MORE IMPORTANTLY, KEEP ON TOP OF THE PLAN. HAVE EACH DRIVER REPORT ON THE PROGRESS.

CREATE A FAMILY ATMOSPHERE: HAVE FUN

Customers like doing business with *positive* people.

As discussed earlier, an average employee spends three-quarters of their wakeful hours preparing for their jobs, transporting themselves to the job site and physically working. Wouldn't you say if you dedicate that much of your life to your job that you'd like to enjoy it? Most human beings are likeable, loveable and fun-loving. Oh, sure, you get the odd grouch. You may even have a cynic or two who predict doom and gloom at every corner. These people are the biggest challenge to motivate. Sometimes it's beyond the scope of a company's ability and professional help is needed. However, I've watched grouches and cynics turn from sour-pusses into nice people! The secret? A Leader who cares.

When you see your staff smiling constantly, when they accomplish their jobs with zest and responsibility and when they go that extra mile to make the company successful, *you know they're happy.*

If your staff hasn't displayed these characteristics, don't despair. A few simple tricks will produce great results. These tricks come under the title of caring for your people. Homosapiens are a simple species. They thrive on love and have deep feelings for each other. Think about all the people that you really care about: your spouse, your mother and father, your son or daughter and your best friend. When there is a shared love and respect, caring for each other comes naturally. You can then rely on each other to grow and develop into a stronger unit.

How does this apply to an organization? Treat your employees with respect, care for them, laugh with them, and they will reward you with hard work and loyalty. Chart #6 points out the many ways that can be used to breathe life and fun into your organization. *When your staff succeeds, so do you.*

There are numerous benefits to creating a family atmosphere and having fun in the workplace. Here are eight of the most important ones:

1. Assists in creating a motivating environment in which people can grow
2. Improves morale
3. Encourages innovation and risk-taking
4. Brings people closer and and builds the team
5. Breaks down those glass barriers or walls which exist between management and staff
6. Improves communications by creating a safer environment: people feel more secure and speak up
7. Fosters trust
8. Relieves a tremendous amount of stress (Hallelujah!)

Many of the managers who attend my training workshops say to me: "But Betska, my workload is so heavy. I'm so stressed out. I can't afford the time to dedicate to creating a family atmosphere and having fun." In reality, you can't afford *not* to delegate the job. Appoint a Vice-President of Fun. To be competitive in this decade and beyond, and to increase productivity, true coaches and leaders will use the information in this chapter to inspire their people.

HOW TO BREATHE LIFE AND FUN INTO YOUR ORGANIZATION

- Know your people by name, staff and customers
- Share your organization's dreams with staff and customers
- Ask them to participate in achieving those dreams
- Remember birthdays
- Remember service anniversaries
- Implement a service recognition program
- Provide free counselling services
- Have regular lunchmeet sessions where you communicate new organizational happenings or goals
- Bring in motivational speakers to give your employees a "A Whack on the Side of the Head"*
- Allow staff to decorate their own workspace
- Train your people to be successful
- Get feedback by developing a system in which you listen to your people and take their suggestions seriously (see page 149 "Royal Marketing Academy")
- Implement a recognition and praise program for all categories and levels of employees
- Smile and be happy even when the chips are down — you'll be amazed how it helps solve problems
- Share the wealth — hinge compensation to corporate performance
- Celebrate your organization's birthday every year. Treat everyone to lunch. Have a barbecue, or organize an evening hoedown with spouses/companions/children in attendance
- Car Rally
- Karaoke Night
- Cookie Exchange
- Have a staff lunch with managers serving the lunch
- Put names in a hat — you bring lunch for the name you pick
- Share recipes
- Declare a "Non-Stress Day"

* also the title of a book by Roger von Oech

Continued

Chart #6

- Set up a garden club where members can exchange seeds, cuttings, perennials, etc.
- Christmas desk decorating contest — get everyone in the spirit!
- Have an annual summer picnic and encourage 100% attendance
- Play puzzles and games at lunchtime
- Organize baseball, bowling, hockey teams
- Show humorous training videos (John Cheese)
- If you're large enough, organize your own day-care program. If you're small, consider joining forces with other organizations
- A well-organized Chinese auction could generate big bucks for charity
- Appraise your staff fairly. Promote only those who deserve to be promoted
- Prior to Christmas, name an Arts and Crafts/Hobby show by employees
- Produce a company newsletter with humorous stories, pictures of employees, training tips, etc.
- All new employees should be introduced by a polaroid picture and bio on the bulletin board
- Have a talent show where employees provide the talent
- Organize your Christmas party — give out awards that poke fun at different things that happened over the year. Have dances where everyone exchanges partners
- Invite the families of staff in tour the plant
- Educate everyone on your products and services — make them proud of your company
- Take photographs of feet — award prizes to people who guess the owners of the feet!
- Implement short- and long-term incentive programs to boost activity and create teamwork
- White elephant sales
- Provide each employee with some slack time — it allows them time to be creative
- Allow longer lunches one day per month
- Show your employees that you care about them, their families and their futures
- Implement a job-sharing program for employees who wish to work parttime
- Send important letters to the homes of staff. Attach an envelope and encourage comments from spouses and children. Answer each letter
- When parting company with employees who don't perform, do so gracefully. Allow them to exit with pride
- Appoint a Vice-President of Fun who will execute all or some of the above

Chart #6

BUILD THE TEAM - CHALLENGE THEM TO BUILD A FUTURE

> "Tough times never last but tough people do."
> — Unknown

A team is a group of people in which members assume specialized roles in doing work while maintaining the cohesiveness and morale of the group. Sounds easy, doesn't it? Sometimes you may think that you have a team and then something happens to put a chip into the strength of your team. For the Leader of an organization, building a team is a tough job. Once it's built, the Leader must be careful to keep it strong and productive.

Before we go on, read through Chart #7 of this section. The chart lists 15 characteristics of an effective team. All of us have had to work in teams during our careers. Things usually got done but if all of these 14 characteristics were not present, the road to accomplishment was usually marred by frustration and resentment. There are a few of these characteristics that must be in place right off the bat and, subsequently, the remaining characteristics will easily fall into being. Let me give you an example of what I mean.

I have heard many appaling or sad stories from the people who attend our training programs. The following is a story of how *not* to build a team. Last year, an international company fired its European V.P. ''Sam'' was, in my opinion, a brilliant businessman. I believe he was fired after continual declines in sales and profits — which were not his fault. He wasn't given the right products for the European market. In any event, Sam was replaced by ''Nick'' from Atlanta, Georgia, who moved to Brussels to head up the European operations. Soon after, Nick called a meeting of all the directors from each European country. He first made them all wait outside a conference room. and then asked them to walk in, single file. In the middle of the room was a coffin! Each director was asked to look inside the coffin: at the bottom of which was a mirror. Once they had all filed passed and sat down, he opened the meeting with the following words: ''The person you saw reflected at the bottom of the coffin is directly responsible for the demise of this company in Europe.'' Nick's conduct was deplorable! How do you think those directors felt? How do you think the directors treated their staff back home? What effect do you think this had on the customer?

**WHEN CUSTOMERS SENSE POOR TEAMWORK,
THEY MAY TAKE THEIR BUSINESS ELSEWHERE.**

TEAM PLANNING

There are many benefits to team planning:
- ☑ improved teamwork
- ☑ mutual understanding
- ☑ better knowledge of company vision
- ☑ issues are addressed

☑ you see the total business
☑ improved communications
☑ puts life into the evaluation process of issues
☑ improved attitudes
☑ more fun

There's that three letter word again — fun! Teams can be fun and productive at the same time.

TEAM GROUND RULES

There are certain ground rules that need to be followed for effective team planning:

☑ everyone contributes
☑ everyone listens and understands
☑ conflicts between ideas are welcomed
☑ avoid arguing to ''win'' (the world is full of people who surface think)
☑ avoid voting, averaging and random choice, think things through
☑ use logic and the most recent, relevant information available
☑ everyone is responsible for the decisions and results

Consensus-seeking among team players is not a majority rule: it is where everyone at least partially agrees with each decision.

During your team planning-sessions, use good brainstorming techniques:

☑ no criticism allowed
☑ free association is okay
☑ try for quantity versus quality ideas
☑ combine and improve on each other's ideas
☑ try to be different and creative
☑ reach for the new and unfamiliar — get off the treadmill
☑ use exaggeration and humor to push ideas beyond familiar limits

---

**HUMOR IS THE SHORTEST DISTANCE
BETWEEN TWO PEOPLE**

A study, by the Wilson Learning Corp., of 4,500 teams in 500 organizations listed the following seven barriers to teamwork.

1. *Rewards and Compensations*
   80% of the respondents indicated that rewards and compensation are based on individual performance versus teams. As a result, the team has little incentive to perform well. Personal agendas take over.
2. *Appraisal Systems*
   A very small percentage of respondents confirmed that the employees were evaluated on team performance during their annual reviews.
3. *Poor Communication from the Top*
   Employees don't know the Mission/Vision/Goals of the organization.
4. *Trust*
   Most managers felt that they couldn't trust their employees to make decisions as a team without management approval.
5. *Organizational Structure*
   The structure encourages internal competition when we should be fighting external competition.
6. *Personal Agendas*
   Some individuals are on a power trip.
7. *Lack of skills*
   Many teams members are not trained how to be a teamplayer.

Other barriers include egos and different values, cultures and beliefs. Take a moment to write a "W" beside the barriers that exist in your organization. Then, put a plan into action to overcome them.

CHARACTERISTICS OF AN EFFECTIVE TEAM

- Clear understanding of the organization's goals.

- High degree of communication between members.

- Effective decision-making methods.

- High degree of trust between members.

- High level of support between members (no back-stabbing).

- Flexibility in procedures.

- Good balance between productivity as a group and as an individual.

- Good balance between rational and emotional-based behaviours.

- Sensitivity to each other's feelings.

- Understanding of each other's strengths and weaknesses.

- Shared leadership among the members - no one member is more important than the other.

- No cliques or domination by any one member.

- Utilization of each member's experience and unique resources.

- High degree of cohesiveness.

- Objective in evaluating their progress as a team.

Chart #7

LISTEN TO YOUR PEOPLE—CAN YOU HEAR WHAT THEY'RE SAYING?

Listening is the art of physically hearing someone else's thoughts and opinions, understanding what they're saying and considering change as a result of it.
— Betska K-Burr

Did you know that we spend 45% of our time listening, 30% of our time speaking, 16% of our time reading and 9% of our time writing? We are taught the reverse order in school. Because we aren't trained to listen, most of us find it hard to listen. In fact, most of us don't realize that we're not listening properly.

Did you also know that we speak at a rate of 120 to 150 words per minute and think at a rate of 500 to 1000 words per minute? *We listen four times faster than we talk.* It is no small wonder that we miss a lot of what people say. In addition, there are many barriers to listening:
- Physical fatigue
- Distractions from surroundings as well as from the speaker (dress, mannerisms)
- Emotional hot buttons
- Bias, perceptions, cultural differences
- Daydreaming, internal thoughts

Most of us practise selective listening. We hear what we want to hear. We remember what we want to remember. To confuse things even more, human beings listen at three different levels. We listen in spurts, then tune in and out. (You can actually see people doing this.) Or, we hear sounds and words only. In effect, we are listening for content only not for the feelings or emotions behind the content. The third level is active listening where we listen for both content and feelings and put ourself in the other's place. Which one of these levels do you use with your spouse? With your children? With the people at work?

Chart #8 is a marvelous tool for improving your listening skills. Used together, these pointers will develop better listening habits that could last you a lifetime. It's best to start now; otherwise, you'll never know what you're missing.

Now that you've improved your skills, how are you going to put them to good work? There are numerous ways to listen to your people:

- ☑ listen well to your managers all the way through the organization at meetings and one-on-one
- ☑ listen to all the employees via suggestion boxes, newsletters, field trips, incentive programs (see index for "The Royal Marketing Academy")
- ☑ listen by walking around and talking to your people and to your customers — ask lots of questions
- ☑ listen via a third party, have an outside company research your organization on its strengths and weaknesses

In *Passion for Excellence*, Peters and Austin write on the principle of Management By Wandering Around or MBWA. "MBWA: the technology of the obvious. It is being in touch with customers, suppliers, your people. It facilitates innovation, and makes possible the teaching of values to every member of an organization. Listening, facilitating, and teaching and reinforcing values. What is this except leadership? Thus, MBWA is the technology of leadership."

COMMUNICATION

How do we go about improving the communication in the workplace? When I ask that question in our training workshops, people often respond with the words: "newsletters," "suggestion boxes" and "hotlines." These can be valuable — no question. However, communication tools such as these elicit superficial responses. Real communication works at two levels: head to head and heart to heart.

HOW TO IMPROVE YOUR LISTENING SKILLS

1. Find areas of interest. Ask yourself, "What's in this for the organization?"

2. Judge the content not the delivery. Nervousness can often affect the delivery.

3. Don't judge the speaker's content before you understand it.

4. Listen for ideas and central themes.

5. Practise taking fewer, but more concise, notes.

6. Work hard at listening. Show them you're interested.

7. Tune out distractions. (Don't answer the phone in the middle of your meeting.)

8. Exercise your mind to relate their information to the organization.

9. Keep an open mind.

10. Capitalize on the fact that thought is faster than speech. Mentally weigh the facts and summarize your thoughts.

Chart #8

Some of the following ideas may be disconcerting to you — but, nobody said that this new leadership paradigm would be easy! You'll note that each method embraces the Yo-Yo Principle or bottom-to-top, top-down communication.

1. Staff Presents at Meetings
   The manager simply opens the meeting, recognizes and praises the team and talks about how far the team has come with respect to the mission/vision/goals of the organization. Once the manager sits down, each employee makes a formal presentation on his or her own opportunities, challenges and goals. This process empowers the staff and makes them feel a part of the team giving them accountability, keeping them focussed and increasing productivity.

2. Evaluations of Management by Staff

3. Evaluations of Peers by Peers

4. Electronic Meetings
   (Sears, Royal Trust and IBM use this method to improve communications.) Basically, every employee sits in front of a computer and answers questions. The benefit is that everyone contributes.

5. A Marketing Council
   (see page 149 ''The Royal Marketing Academy'') This superb program keeps the Ivory Tower in touch with the employees.

6. The Personal Profile System
   How can we possibly manage people if we don't understand ourselves? How can we possibly be strong team players if we don't understand each other? The Personal Profile System (DISC) is a powerful team builder. It tells us what motivates Sally and what demotivates Jim. If you haven't taken the DISC, order one today. (see page 235)

SHARE THE WEALTH - HINGE COMPENSATION TO PERFORMANCE

> "**A**ll successful employers are stalking men who will do the unusual, men who think, men who attract attention by performing more than is expected of them."
> — Charles M. Schwab

Today, we stalk both men and women who are hard-working, creative and who go that extra mile. These are the people who get things done, who make decisions and who come up with brilliant ideas. Then, there are employees who simply put in an 8 hour day, who follow their job description to the "T" and then go home. Flashes of creative genius are few and far between. Which type of employee is the most valuable to your organization? The answer is that they are both valuable. The dynamos are required to bring continual effervescence to your organization. The steady workers will keep the machinery running smoothly.

What does all this have to do with "sharing the wealth"? Will the dynamos and steady workers work harder, faster and better if you hinge compensation to company performance? Psychologists would probably answer that question with a question: What motivates an individual to perform outside the norm? Some are motivated by money, others by an opportunity to advance their careers and the remainder by recognition.

> **PEOPLE ARE MOTIVATED BY 3 SIMPLE NEEDS:**
> **MONEY, OPPORTUNITY, RECOGNITION**

There are groups of people who are motivated by all three needs and others who work hard only to obtain an opportunity for career advancement. A very important question now arises: Can you motivate someone whose primary need is not money by hinging compensation to company performance? The answer is yes. Money is always a motivator even if it is a secondary need. Do you know of anyone who has refused extra money in their pay cheques? But let's look deeper into this topic since it is such a controversial one.

My belief is that everyone in the organization contributes to the generation of sales and the making of profits. Take the receptionist: if the receptionist is on a bonus program tied to the company's performance of sales and profits, he or she can do many things to affect company performance, such as:

- use supplies sparingly
- be deterred from pilfering company supplies for home use
- drum up sales leads from family, friends, acquaintances
- project a positive image. The receptionist is often the first person a prospect contacts in the organization. His or her attitude can affect a prospect's decision on whether or not to do business with your company.
- if your receptionist also handles paperwork such as receivables, he or she can ensure fast processing of the monies that can affect profits

The list can go on and on. At the end of the quarter when the bonus cheque arrives, the receptionist will feel proud of his or her contribution to the success of the company. To a degree, all employees have a sense of being master of their own fate. This feeling is intensified as you climb the ladder to where major decisions are made which have a greater impact on sales and profits. To a greater degree, these managers are masters of their own fate.

Already more than 50 percent of medium-to-large companies are experimenting with some form of variable compensation for non-executives. From management's perspective, the primary purpose of "pay for performance" (PFP) programs is to change an organization's corporate culture and focus employee effort on specific behavioral and business goals. It's possible to effect innovation with PFP. Employees will also begin to think and act more like owners of the business rather than hirelings who simply put in their time. PFP can build teamwork. I've watched administrative staff question the purchases requested by other departments. "Do you need that many widgets?" "Can I suggest a less expensive supplier?" PFP enhances communication between employees.

The development of a PFP plan needs careful consideration. Let me share with you two examples of PFP plans — one that is working well and one that didn't. One industrial company in Vancouver, B.C. hires young recruits in their twenties from the British Columbia Institute of Technology. These young employees average $50,000 a year and more because, in addition to paying them $15 per hour, the company shares 35% of its profit after the first $200,000. This means that each employee received a profit-sharing cheque of $18,000 in 1987 and $25,000 in 1988. The company was willing to share their success with the people who worked so hard to make it happen.

Another company, this one in the textile business, had a rough experience with a PFP launched in 1988. It involved 15,000 blue-collar and 5,000 white-collar workers in its fibres business unit. The plan appeared to be fair, with a potential payoff of up to 18% bonus. Unfortunately, the industry experienced adverse conditions. The employees were not willing to accept the fact that there would be times when external factors such as economic downturns would affect their pay regardless of how hard they themselves had worked. When times were good, they liked the bonuses. When times were bad, they didn't appreciate the risk involved in a PFP plan.

Allan Owen of Owen Production Consultants (London, Ontario) is a highly sought-after specialist in the design of gain-sharing programs. He says that "the prime difference between pure profit sharing and gain sharing is:

1) the measurement is typically based on those measures that are directly controlled by the employees, and;

2) the bonus is paid out either monthly or quarterly with gain sharing (as opposed to annually with a profit-sharing plan).

Alan and I both agree that gain-sharing programs can be used by both the public and private sector to increase and maintain productivity. The measurement in both sectors could be based on any number of factors. Here are a few: the number of customer complaints, length of time to fix a complaint, ideas generated, customer waiting time, number of repeat customer complaints, number of trees that get clipped, etc. Alan believes that "successful gain-sharing plans measure what counts, communicates what counts, and pays for what counts."

Chart #9 summarizes the numerous benefits to sharing the wealth. When your staff succeeds, so do you.

HINGING COMPENSATION TO COMPANY PERFORMANCE

— 9 BIG BENEFITS —

- Changes the corporate culture — everyone feels important to the company's success

- Focuses employee effort on specific behavioral and business goals

- Effects innovation

- Inspires a feeling of ownership by each employee — they think and act like owners rather than hirelings who simply put in time

- Builds teamwork — everyone helps each other to do a better job

- Enhances communication between employees

- Encourages everyone to be responsible for sales and profits

- Employees pull together spiritually during tough times to ride out the storm

- Builds loyalty to the organization

Chart #9

MAKE RECOGNITION AND PRAISE A WAY OF LIFE—BE PROUD OF THEIR EFFORTS

Before you can build an effective team, everyone must feel *equally important* to the organization.

Michael LeBoeuf, author of *the Greatest Management Principle in the World*, verbalizes the above quote in another way. "The things that get rewarded get done." GMP teaches us to ensure that we reward the right behaviors. It's also important to be consistent with how you reward your people. I can recall one instance where the reward was given for the correct behavior but was given to one employee only when others deserved rewards as well. In this story, the employee had been working multiple hours of overtime for months in order to complete a major project. Others around him had also been putting in long, long hours on the same project and on other unrelated projects. The company was in a start-up operation where the employees were all gung-ho to make their new company successful. The teamwork and cooperation was a sight to behold. At the end of the major project, the employee who had been working multiple hours of overtime was rewarded with a computer printer for his home. The presentation was made in front of his peers who had also busted their behinds to get things done. In the end, the peers became demotivated. They wondered why they were not rewarded for their efforts. What effect do you think this situation had on the future work output and attitude of the other employees? Here's the lesson:

REWARD THE RIGHT BEHAVIOURS AND BE CONSISTENT WITH THE WAY YOU REWARD BEHAVIOURS.

LeBoeuf in the *GMP* details the ten behaviours to reward and ten behaviours not to reward:

REWARD	INSTEAD OF
1. Solid solutions	1. Quick fixes
2. Risk taking	2. Risk avoiding
3. Applied creativity	3. Mindless comformity
4. Decisive action	4. Paralysis by analysis
5. Smart work	5. Busywork
6. Simplification	6. Needless complication
7. Quietly effective behaviour	7. Squeaking joints
8. Quality work	8. Fast work
9. Loyalty	9. Turnover
10. Working together	10. Working against

There are numerous ways to reward good behaviour. Chart #10 separates them out into the three categories MONEY - OPPORTUNITY - RECOGNITION. The least expensive rewards fall under the ''Opportunity'' section. These rewards provide the individual with an opportunity to grow. They recognize him/her for a job well done by trusting him/her to take on more responsibility and more authority.

If we were to survey a broad range of employees, I'm sure the majority would agree that rewards which are intangible and those which show sincere thought and consideration have a much longer-lasting effect.

In setting up your reward program, begin by setting performance goals. Then choose the rewards that are best suited to the goal.

MAKING PEOPLE FEEL LIKE WINNERS
— The Rewards —

MONEY	OPPORTUNITY	RECOGNITION
• Raise • Subscription to professional publication • Paid time for self improvement • Favorable overtime • Bonus • Free passes to events • Health club memberships • Time off with pay • Membership in civic organizations • Taken out for lunch or dinner with spouse • Prizes • Stock ownership • Travel • Six weeks holiday on the 10th year of service • Staff discount • $ to decorate workspace • Control over budget • Training tapes/books • Gift certificates • RSPs	• Increased responsibility • Outside training • Increased authority • Flex time • Opportunity to set own goals • Become a group leader • Promotion based on performance • Cross-training • Delegate more • Task force assignments • Participation in management meetings • Freedom to choose how to accomplish tasks • Make them supervisor for the day • Appointments to boards or associations • Specialization by individuals • Cross-pollination (Short-term job change)	• Specific praise and reinforcement • Certificates, plaques, trophies, rings, pins • Employee-of-the-month awards • Personal nameplate/ badge • Personalized business cards • Photo in company newsletter • Photo in annual report • Photo in local newspaper • Memo in file for good performance • Allow personalization of work area • Title change • Acknowledgement on special days by peers • Special parking spot • Privacy in work space • Picture in Hall of Fame • Send copy of memo home to spouse

Chart #10

> **WHEN PERFORMANCE IS WITHIN ACCEPTABLE RANGES OF GOALS SET FOR THE JOB, USE REWARDS TO INCREASE AND SUSTAIN POSITIVE PERFORMANCE AND PERSONAL MOTIVATION.**

Why do you think we as homosapiens have difficulty in giving effective recognition and praise? Some reasons might be: we have received it as children; we were never taught how to do it; thoughts of manipulation; patronization; misinterpretation or sexual come-ons may cross our minds. What we tend to forget is this:

> **EMPLOYEES WILL GO OUT OF THEIR WAY TO DO A GREAT JOB, IF WE THANK THEM.**

There is not a single soul alive today who does not like to receive praise. Some prefer to receive it in private, others bask in the glory of recognition in front of their peers. To avoid embarrassment, make sure you know how comfortable your recipients will feel about praise in public.

The following three quick steps to giving praise are most effective:

1. Say thank you. "Sally I'd like to thank you for completing Project XYZ."
2. Give detail: "You went to the library to research the material, did the analysis then communicated the results to your colleagues."
3. Describe behavior. "I appreciate your attention to detail and your ability to communicate. Thank you again."

In summary, make recognition and praise a part of your organization's culture. Be proud of the efforts of your people. Let them know that you know how well they are performing. *When your staff succeeds, so do you.*

DELEGATE AUTHORITY AND RESPONSIBILITY —TRUST YOUR PEOPLE

> **S**how me an employee who doesn't like to have the freedom to make decisions and I'll eat my hat.

I'm willing to bet that most of you have had the experience of working for managers with varying management styles. I've certainly experienced a potpourri of management personalities and styles in my time. The best managers were the ones who cared about my progress, who delegated responsibility and who trusted me enough to give me authority to make decisions. The managers that caused me the greatest grief were the ones who trusted no one. They delegated responsibility but refused to give their managers any decision-making power. Those were frustrating times. However, every problem is brilliantly disguised as an opportunity. I learned how debilitating that management style was to an organization's progress. These managers think that a successful executive is one who can delegate all the responsibility, shift all the blame and appropriate all the credit!

The Democratic Manager is the one who will make your organization run smoothly while maximizing the company's ability to reach sales and profit goals. Chart #11 provides a host of techniques that can be used to motivate people through delegating authority and responsibility. Perhaps the most important technique is designing a job description that communicates the employee's responsibilities and level of authority. The job description should include the expected measurable results, ie; Report A is to be completed by the second working day of each month. Each employee must fully understand what is expected of them. We can use the same expression here that we used in Application #2...if you don't know where you're going, how are you going to get there?

Along with delegating responsibility and authority comes clear, open communication. By practising MBWA, you will be accessible to them. Encourage employees to express their opinions. Show them how they fit into your organization's goals. Consistently let them know how well they're doing compared to their goals. Keep them informed on the progress of the company's goals. Give them as much advance notice of changes as possible.

Cooperation, interest and support cannot be forced from your people — it must be earned. Every employee needs to feel needed. They need to feel important. They need to know the significance of their job on the overall scheme of things.

EVERY EMPLOYEE NEEDS TO FEEL NEEDED.

Now, it's time to take some personal inventory. Are you a Democratic Manager or an Autocratic Manager? Ask your people what they think. Show them Chart #11. Ask them how many of these techniques you use in managing them. It's tough to receive this kind of feedback. You'll be amazed at what you find out. Ask them to help you change for the better and you will grow as a Manager. Moreover, your employees will respect you for it.

DELEGATING AUTHORITY AND RESPONSIBILITY

— TECHNIQUES FOR EMPOWERING EMPLOYEES —

☐ trust your employees to do their jobs to the best of their ability

☐ delegate responsibility; be available to coach them

☐ delegate authority; let them know the types of decisions that they can make, the level of signing authority for money, etc.

☐ provide understudy training; let them know you want them to grow

☐ appoint employees as members of special committees, task forces, special projects

☐ use your people as "inside experts"; ask their opinions

☐ have direct reports fill in as vacation replacements for managers

☐ include employees in discussion to solve job-related problems

☐ schedule employees as instructors, trainers and meeting leaders

☐ involve employees in setting goals, business plans and schedules

☐ have employees accompany you or represent you at meetings, internally and externally

☐ use job rotation to increase knowledge, responsibility and authority

☐ schedule employees for specific training

☐ conduct regular employee performance appraisals to give positive feedback and assist with personal growth

☐ encourage development plans/training during off hours

☐ redesign jobs to match up with the real abilities of each person

☐ design a job description for each employee that clarifies responsibilities in terms of realistic measures of quality performance

☐ assign tasks that really challenge (stretch) each employee

☐ reward the results of job performance

☐ ask for employee feedback on how you are doing as a manager

Chart #11

TRAIN YOUR PEOPLE - INVEST IN YOUR FUTURE

> "The more high technology around us, the more the need for human touch."
> — *Megatrends*

According to Tom Peters, co-author of *In Search of Excellence*, one of the companies he researches spends four full days training their parking lot attendants. The employees are usually teenagers who work for a grand total of 5 weeks! The company is Disneyland. Those of you who have had the pleasure of visiting a Disney location know that this organization exemplifies true customer service. In their opinion, the parking lot attendant is often the first person park guests meet. Like a receptionist in an office, the attendants reflect the personality of the organization. Hire a grumpy receptionist and you'll have customers and suppliers questioning whether or not they should be doing business with you.

Poor training is also one of the main reasons why good employees leave. During tough economic times, advertising and training are the two areas that companies cut. Once again, that short-term thinking puts us in a panic.

Tom Peters has some wise words for us on training, "The excellent companies view extensive, pragmatic training as a necessity, not as a boom-time nicety...you gotta trust 'em, and train the livin' daylights out of them.''.

There are a few ways in which you can train your people:
1. Spend time with them - teach them a lot of what you know.
2. Call upon other employees to train your people.
3. Hire trainers to conduct workshops for your employees on-site.
4. Send your employees off-site for training (good interaction with employees from other organizations).
5. Encourage your employees to take courses on their own time.
6. Cross-pollinate your people; ie; put accountants into marketing and marketing into warehousing for 6 months or a year or longer.

To paraphrase the beginning quote from Megatrends, the rampant use of computerized systems has often left us feeling isolated and in need of the human touch. I can think of one example that makes me frustrated just thinking about it. Many organizations now have these diabolical computerized voices that answer their phone. The tape will go something like this, ''If you would like to speak to a customer service rep, press 1. If you would like to order product, press 2. If you have any billing questions, press 3.'' I don't mind the short ones, they're often a necessity, but the messages that go on and on forever drive me nuts. I recently phoned one organization to find that no where on the tape was their an opportunity to get some general information. I learned later that all you have to do is stay on the line and an operator will take your call. In the meantime, I had to call another number just to figure out how to use the main number! These computerized voice answering systems do not replace the warmth and friendliness of a human being. As discussed earlier, the receptionist projects the image of your organization. Whenever I receive a computerized voice, I think of an organization which is cold and uncaring and not too concerned about customer service. You cannot train a machine to be warm and caring (yet).

One of the main jobs of a Leader is to develop his/her people to be successful. Training in your organization's specific products/services and in general business is a must. However, there are some other deeper thoughts that should be taught to your employees. Chart #12 points out the often forgotten skills which employees today must have in order to be stronger employees in both mind and spirit. These are skills that you don't learn in our educational systems. Yet, these are the skills that everyone needs if they want to be good employees; more so, if they want to climb the ladder.

Technique number one, ''confidence'', is a skill that so many people lack. I want to tell you a story about a young lady whom I had inherited once as a a manager. Sally (not her real name) had been a wife and mother for approximately 7 years. Upon entering the workforce she became a secretary and thought that she was to remain a secretary. Sally lacked confidence because she only had a high school education. Not many of these women realize that being a mother and running a household for several years is equivalent to a college degree. In running a good home, you have to be an exceptional manager. You develop outstanding organizational skills, you do the family's finance, you make plans for the future, you coach your children how to be decent human beings, you have a heavy workload, and you have to be a team player.

Sally hadn't worked for me very long before I realized that she had more potential. It took me a few months to boost her confidence and to encourage her to upgrade her computer and general business skills through training. It took a lot of coaching on my part to make her realize that she could climb the ladder without a college degree. Frankly, she had better organizational skills, more gut instinct, far better people skills and was more creative than some of the MBA's I've known! Today, Sally is flourishing as a Marketing Coordinator. All it took was a little confidence.

John Naisbitt, author of *Megatrends*, knows the value of human touch in managing people. Train them in the technical skills that they need in which to do the job. More importantly, teach them the skills that they need to shape their minds and spirits. These are the skills that will make them successful. *When your staff succeeds, so do you.*

TRAINING THE MIND AND THE SPIRIT

— 20 TECHNIQUES TO PERSONAL SUCCESS —

1. **YOU BECOME WHAT YOU THINK ABOUT**
   Have confidence, believe in yourself.

2. **DECIDE WHAT YOU WANT IN LIFE**
   Write out personal goals. What are you going to do to get there?

3. **HAVE COURAGE**
   Don't let the fear of failure hold you back. Failure is success if we learn from it.

4. **HAVE INTEGRITY**
   Be true to yourself - listen to your intuition. Don't be afraid to admit you're wrong.

5. **BE POSITIVE**
   Attitude versus aptitude determines altitude.

6. **LEARN HOW TO COMMUNICATE**
   Learn writing skills, public speaking and selling skills. Be cheerful. Have positive expectations.

7. **ACQUIRE A SENSE OF URGENCY**
   Develop a reputation for speed with quality work. Set priorities and follow through.

8. **MAKE CUSTOMER SERVICE A PASSION**
   Your boss, your peers, your distributors and suppliers, prospects and the end-user are all your customers. Give them world-class quality service.

9. **BE WILLING TO WORK HARD**
   Go outside the job description - go the extra mile. Accept 100% responsibility for your work. Do jobs no one else wants.

Continued. . .

Chart #12

10. **CONTINUALLY UPGRADE YOUR SKILLS**
Take courses, block off time to read, listen to tapes, volunteer to head task forces.

11. **NETWORK**
Join breakfast meetings, professional and community groups. Make a valuable contribution.

12. **BECOME AN EXPERT**
Information is power. Become an expert in your job.

13. **MANAGE YOUR LIFE**
Balancing your career and personal life is a must. Find a balance with spirituality, physical exercise, close family and friends and a vision of what you want to be.

14. **BE A PLANNER**
Develop a reputation for being a planner, for thinking ahead 3 to 20 years. Put plans on paper. Strive for the organization's goal.

15. **BE CREATIVE**
Use both right and left brain skills to create new ideas and new programs, and to increase sales and reduce costs.

16. **BE A TEAMPLAYER**
Trust the people around you, support them, make everyone feel important. No back-stabbing.

17. **DRESS FOR SUCCESS**
Dress for the job but make a statement.

18. **CONTROL YOUR FUTURE**
Ask for a promotion or to head a new project. Look for all opportunities to learn.

19. **HELP OTHER PEOPLE GROW**
Become a mentor and a coach. When other people succeed, so do you.

20. **BE A NICE PERSON**
It's nice to be important but it's more important to be nice.

Chart #12

ESTABLISH A GREAT CUSTOMER SERVICE PROGRAM—YOUR BACKBONE FOR THE '90s AND INTO THE 21st CENTURY

> **I**f your customers reach the future before you do, you may get left behind.

Every manager has a certain amount of responsibility for marketing. Moreover, every employee has a responsibility for servicing the customer. If a company's products or services cannot be sold, then the business will obviously fail. If an organization is losing its current customer base, chances are the customers aren't being well treated. If you're having trouble in both areas, cast your feelers out to the people within your organization. Are they happy?

Let's back up a minute here to define a very important word - CUSTOMER. To whom do we apply the term? You may be surprised to learn that every organization, public or private, has 5 sets of customers. First, you have *end-user customers* who are using your product and/or service as we speak. Secondly, *prospects* are your future customers. Sell them on your company and its products and/or services and they will become part of your database. The third type of customer is your *distributors*. Some will buy products from you or simply act as agents to sell your products/services to the end-user. Since distributors buy from you, they are your customer. The fourth type of customer is your *suppliers*. They can supply you with that product that you sell or simply supply you with office equipment, paper, pens, widgets or services with which to run your operation. You are their customer and they are yours. The fifth type of customer is your *employees*. They supply each other with a service, helping each other to turn a smooth operation.

The employees are the *internal* customers, the other 4 are *external* customers.

WHO IS "THE CUSTOMER"?

1. **CURRENT END-USERS**
2. **PROSPECTS**
3. **DISTRIBUTORS**
4. **SUPPLIERS**
5. **EMPLOYEES**

In short, *a customer is anyone with whom you come into contact in the course of doing your job.*

Each one of these customers will be dealt with in some detail in this section. As you read through, you will encounter ideas that can be used to set up customer service programs in all 5 areas. They all fall under one umbrella program which I call C.A.R.E.

C. A. R. E.
Customer Assurance Reaches Everywhere

Isn't that what customer service is all about - caring? Customer service or customer assurance, as many people call it, doesn't just reach out to the end-user. Many of the programs you see in use today were developed for the end-user only. The reality is that the same service and the same caring must reach out to prospects, distributors, suppliers and employees. If any member of the Group of 5 customers (herein called the G5) is disgruntled, the other four groups will be affected. *Customer assurance reaches everywhere.*

For the C.A.R.E. program to work effectively, a clear statement of its importance must be made by the Chief Executive Officer in order to mobilize a total corporate commitment. That reminds me of another story told to me by a client. Company x launched a customer service program with beautiful posters and pins. The launch came from the Marketing Dept. where most creative pieces originate. Two things stultified the program. First, the C.E.O. should have made a statement about the significance of the program and launched it under his signature. Secondly, without a detailed training program, the employees were not trained in the art of customer service. All they had were beautiful posters and pins that meant nothing to them.

C.A.R.E. FOR THE END-USER CUSTOMER

In the past, some companies have succeeded despite themselves. In selected markets, they were able to get away with poor service. Today, the market place is not as kind and usually deals quickly and unforgivingly with poor service companies. They simply go elsewhere. The competitiveness in the nineties will be the most fierce in recent history. Even given the fact that you are an excellent company with strong R & D efforts, good pricing and great products, poor service hits the gossip fan quicker than rats multiply. And that's fast!

Let's clarify another point here before we go too far. *CARE-ing for the end-user customer is everyone's responsibility* - not just sales and marketing. From the receptionist through to the delivery man, every employee touches the life of the end-user customer.

Here are the steps to follow in developing and implementing C.A.R.E. for the end-user:

1. GET CLOSE TO THE CUSTOMER
Visit several customers, tour their facilities, ask questions, sit in on their meetings, attend their own conferences and those of their industry.

Solicit ideas from the employees on the front line who deal directly with the end-users.

Or, have a third party consulting company do the research for you, although it's a good exercise to do it yourself. The P.R. alone is worth the effort.

While you're out there, ask 3 important questions of your customers:
- Why did you buy from us?
- What do you want us to continue doing?
- What can we do to better service you?

Since head office and administrative staff are in touch with the customer regularly for re-orders and billings, have them visit the customer at least once per year. These employees can also ask the same questions and come back with suggestions.

2. DEVELOP THE PROGRAM

Now that you've got a pot full of ideas, what are you going to do with them? One of the benefits of third party research is that a statistical analysis will prioritize the customer's needs. Quantitative research in the form of focus panels can also prioritize for you.

Let's say, for example, that most of your customers wanted a 1-800 # for 24 hour service, a one hour delivery service for supplies and the option to request a replacement product if their current one keeps breaking down. The Sears people truly understand their customers. The Sears guarantee is "Satisfaction or money refunded" - clean and simple and effective. Design your program around customer needs. You'll need to consider designing 6 parts to the program:

(1) A brochure with all the details including an individual guarantee, if necessary.

(2) A video directed to the prospect informing them of the commitment of your company to service. Your sales people should use this as a selling tool.

(3) Posters, hanging or stand-alone point-of-purchase displays, buttons, decals and whatever you need to tell the world about your C.A.R.E. program. Put it on your business cards, your stationery, brochures and advertising vehicles. Use as many communications vehicles as possible to reach out and touch the customer.

(4) An internal package including a letter from the CEO selling the employees on the importance of the program and their role in it.

(5) An on-going communication program with your end-users. Develop a computerized end-user database which can be manipulated to analyze your base. You should become very intimate with your customers. American Express does an outstanding job with database marketing. They know

the demographic and psychographics of their customers inside and out. It wouldn't surprise me if they knew how many of their end-users had gold teeth!

Once you have your database, send correspondence out to them regularly. Put your organization's name in front of their face on a regular basis. Postcards announcing new products or discount sales are good vehicles. Try coupons. A newsletter with "tips" is also a hit.

(6) A good recovery program. To err is human and computers do a good job of it as well! Even if an employee never flubs his lines when it comes to handling customer complaints, there will be times when needs and expectations fail to mesh to everyone's satisfaction. In such cases, its crucial to address customer problems as quickly and as completely as possible. Employees and distributors must work hard to "recover" angry customers. Find out what happens now when you have an angry customer. Does anyone apologize? Who attempts to fix the problem? Once you have the answers, design a good recovery program. Don't let an angry customer leave the fold. He/she usually tells about 10 other people about the episode. You can bet your boots that those 10 won't do business with you either. Here is a quick 5 step recovery plan:

(a) Apologize - sincerely acknowledge the error.

(b) Quick reinstatement - customer must believe that you are doing your best to get things back in order and that you have their best interests at heart.

(c) Empathy - an apology tells the customer it matters that there was a breakdown whereas empathy adds it matters that the person involved was frustrated and irritated.

(d) Atonement - say to the customer that we want to make it up to you. They will want to hear this.

(e) Follow-up - very important to recovery. Both the customer and the front-line employees need to be friends again. Train your employees to follow-up to ensure a happy relationship.

The overall message of a recovery system is this,

WHEN SERVICE FAILS, TREAT THE PERSON, THEN THE PROBLEM.

According to data compiled by the Technical Assistance Research Programs Institute (TARP) in its National Consumer Survey conducted for the U.S. Office of Consumer Affairs, it found that resolving problems quickly and efficiently had a positive impact on customer loyalty. Research showed that consumers who had problems, complained and had their problems satisfactorily resolved were more likely to be brand loyal than consumers without problems and significantly more loyal than customers who experienced problems but failed to register a complaint. Even in instances when the problem was not resolved but the customer felt he had been "listened to," there was an indication they would give the offending company another try.

Other studies have shown that only 4% of unhappy customers will complain, while 96 out of 100 simply switch to the competition! All the more reason to *audit* your customers on a regular basis *to make sure they're happy.*

3. SELLING THE PROGRAM TO YOUR STAFF

Use the tools mentioned above to communicate to your employees the details of your C.A.R.E. package. The best way to launch it would be at your organization's annual convention where all employees could gather. If you have distributors, invite them as well. Ask for feedback from the floor. Answer all questions. Diffuse any negatives by reminding them that the end-user is all important to the longevity of your business. Break the group up into smaller workshops and have them brainstorm on ways that they can use C.A.R.E. to reach their current customer base and prospects. Allow them to have ownership in the program.

4. PROGRAM REVIEW

This step is key to the survival of C.A.R.E. . Between 6 months to a year, go back and visit the same customers you visited in your research days. Ask them what they think of the program and what other improvements they would like to see. Ask your employees and distributors the same question. Make any necessary changes to the program and communicate them to your people. Do an audit like this annually. Customer needs change rapidly. Don't let the competition anywhere near your slice of the pie!

C.A.R.E. FOR THE PROSPECT CUSTOMER

Your customer program for the prospect customer is the same as for the current end-user, with one exception. Obtain the names of all the prospects who bought from the competition - have your sales people collect them. Send these lost sale prospects a questionnaire asking:
1. Why didn't they buy from you and
2) What do you have to do to earn their business the next time they buy.

C. A. R. E.

CUSTOMER ASSURANCE REACHES EVERYWHERE

— 4 STEPS —

1. GET CLOSE TO THE CUSTOMER
   Determine their needs

2. DEVELOP THE PROGRAM
   - Support Material (Videos, Brochures, Pins, Letters, Etc.)
   - Ongoing Communication Program Using A Database System
   - Good Recovery System When the Program Fails

3. SELL THE PROGRAM TO YOUR STAFF (AND DISTRIBUTORS)

4. REVIEW THE PROGRAM REGULARLY

Chart #13

Make sure your salespeople know the real answer to the loss. I've discovered that nine times out of ten the sales force blames the lost sale on price! When we've gone back to the prospect to query the customer, other answers surface: service commitment, product quality, salesmanship, the prospect golfed with the competition, etc.

Now that you have the lost prospect's name on file, flog him or her with mail. Be selective but send him cards on new products or discount sales. Keep your logo in front of his face. When the time comes to buy again, he won't forget you.

Have your salesperson in the territory call on these lost prospects. They should physically keep in touch for the same reason you've kept in touch via the mail...top-of-mind awareness.

C.A.R.E. FOR DISTRIBUTOR AND SUPPLIER CUSTOMERS

C.A.R.E. for these two groups of the G5 is exactly the same as for the end-user customer. Find out their needs, develop the program, sell it to your staff and to the dealer and then review it annually. Keeping these two groups of customers happy is a tough job. See your index for a C.A.R.E. program developed for Dealers: ''Star Reach — A Dealer Program''. In addition to ''Star Reach'' use the same techniques for Distributors (and Suppliers) as described below in the C.A.R.E. Employee Program. After all, they are an extension of your family.

C.A.R.E. FOR THE EMPLOYEE CUSTOMER

This last customer in the G5 should be the first group to receive training in all aspects of customer service. All 5 groups will require proper telephone skills and interpersonal skills. In addition, each department will require skills relevant only to that group. A complete customer service program for employees is the topic of another book; however, I'm including some of the more salient points in summary below. Under each employee category are the training needs specific to that category. The employee customer is divided into three areas for training purposes: service, office and sales personnel.

SERVICE TECHNICIAN
Have you heard the expression, ''Sales start after the sale is made?'' The initial sale is a good start but the toughest job is yet to come.

Your Service Technician is the most influential employee in keeping a customer happy and in a repeat-order frame of mind. If the service tech fails to do the job, you can bet that the customer will soon be out shopping. In order to service the customer well, your service people need to be trained on the following:

— YOUR C.A.R.E. PROGRAM FOR THE END-USER CUSTOMER
  They need to know what the customer and the company expects of them. How frequent should service be needed? How fast should he or she respond? How many calls should he or she be making in a day? Can we define quality? Your techs need to know the level of service of each product, ie; mean time between failures. They also need to know the level of service of each customer. Before a tech calls, he should know the service history of that location. If the calls have been frequent, the end-user customer may need some TLC.

— INTERPERSONAL SKILLS
  Service Techs are usually well-trained in the repair of products. In my experience, though, they are usually a quiet and introverted group of individuals. They are happier tinkering with their tools than talking to people. For this reason, techs need substantial training in dealing with people. Simple training like handling the people aspect of their job when they walk through the door. How to approach the receptionist? Whom they talk to? How to deal with angry customers and leave them with a smile on their face?

Along with the end-user customer, the Service Techs need to learn interpersonal skills with other employees, dealers and suppliers. They require the same training listed below under "Office Personnel."

The Service Technician is your company's key ambassador for after-sale support. Train him or her well.

OFFICE PERSONNEL

In this group, you have a mixture of receptionists, clerks, managers and manufacturing line personnel. They work in different disciplines: order entry, customer service, warehousing, computer database management, marketing, finance, and manufacturing. Once again, they arrive on your doorstep with different personalities. The finance people are usually the conservative number crunchers — the people who hate to take risks. There is also the good-natured, hard-working manufacturing employees who don't interact much with the other disciplines. The marketers, who inherently possess extroverted personalities, are very creative and thrive on taking risks. All of these disciplines, with their varying personalities, need to be taught how to get along with each other and with the other four members of the G5. Train them in their specific job tasks. More importantly, teach them:

— how to inter-relate with end-user customers, suppliers, distributors and prospects
— telephone skills
— how to be a member of the team (See Chart #7)
— how to deal with difficult people
— how to breathe life into your organization (see Chart #6)
— how to set goals and achieve them (see Chart #5)
— how to be a leader (see Chart #3 & 4)
— how to listen (see Chart #8)
— how to delegate authority and responsibility (see Chart #11)
— interviewing, recruiting and selecting skills

The office personnel are the wheels that keep your organization moving from day to day. Develop a solid training program for them. Schedule training for new employees and listen for feedback to ensure change, if change is required.

SALES PERSONNEL

Your salespeople are often the first contact a prospect has with your organization. They, too, are ambassadors. Once they leave the prospect's office, they leave behind an impression of your company. Make sure it's a good one. You want the prospects to remember your company as being professional, caring, knowledgeable and service-oriented. Train your salespeople on your products and services. Teach them how to sell. Teach them about the C.A.R.E. program for the end-user customer. Prepare a sightseller for them — a professional binder that assists the rep in educating the prospect on your company's products and services, company history and why they should buy from you. Whereas the service tech is the introverted employee, the sales rep is the aggressive, often selfish, individual. One of their greatest training needs is the people skills program outlined for office personnel above.

The sales rep must know that once a sale is made the job has just begun. He or she is also responsible for keeping that end-user customer happy.

C.A.R.E. RECOGNITION

Your employees, your distributors and your suppliers should all be recognized for superior service rendered. Designing the programs will take a bit of analysis. There are numerous ways to recognize "Service Heroes." As you recognize your heroes, you'll notice a marked improvement in the quality of service. Once again, set expectations for servicing each group of the G5. Each group will then have goals to reach and will know what is expected of them. .

Design your recognition program to include measurable results. For example, techs can be measured on response times, call backs and quality. Office personnel can be measured on etiquette or ideas for improving customer service. Sales can be measured on the growth of their customer base and retention of customers. Whatever you choose for a recognition program, make sure that it recognizes everyone's efforts. Use your company newsletter to honor your "Service Heroes". See index for "Star Reach - The Newsletter".

SUMMARY

A company known for good customer service not only retains its customers, it can actually afford to charge more for its products. People are willing to pay more when they feel they are getting their money's worth. Service always pays for itself.

To protect your end-user customer base, carefully monitor that side of the business. Watch for any sudden departures of current customers. Find out why they left. Try to prevent any more losses.

As we move further along into this competitive decade and into the 21st century, good end-user customer service will keep your base happy. A happy base tells others about your company and more sales will be generated. Happy employees, distributors and suppliers will strengthen your organization.

IN THE COMPETITIVE 90's AND BEYOND, C.A.R.E.-ING FOR YOUR G5 CUSTOMERS WILL SECURE A FUTURE FOR YOUR ORGANIZATION.

"Your prospects don't care how much you know... until they know how much your care."

PART B:

WHY AND HOW TO CONDUCT SUCCESSFUL RECOGNITION/ INCENTIVE PROGRAMS

WHY AND HOW TO CONDUCT SUCCESSFUL RECOGNITION/ INCENTIVE PROGRAMS

"Sales are up 30% over last year!"
"The company's profit picture is the best it's ever been."
"Our employees seem happier — more motivated."
"Productivity has improved dramatically."

Ah, these improvements are music to any manager's ears! As Leaders, our mandate is to improve the organization's performance. People drive the wheels that move your organization. *Only they* can improve the organization's performance. In Part A, we discussed at length the ten critical applications you need in order to create champions. This chapter deals with the use of incentive programs to motivate employees.

Parts C and D of this book are full of great incentive programs. As a whole, these programs touch all ten applications of *Creating Champions*. Incentive programs will assist you in being a Leader and setting an example. You can use them to communicate goals and create a family atmosphere. Incentives can be awesome team builders. Use them to listen to your people. Incentives can generate higher sales which generate more commission dollars for the sales reps. Recognition and praise are automatic spinoffs of incentive programs. You can use incentives to delegate authority and responsibility and to train your people on new products, for example. Finally, your incentives can be made a part of your C.A.R.E. customer service programs. Incentives are fun ways to focus attention on certain aspects of your business.

Incentive programs should be used to reward people for work done above and beyond the norm and/or in situations where management needs to focus attention on a particular product or service. Incentives alone cannot make people happy. As stated in the opening chapter of this book, incentive programs can assist you in temporarily boosting morale. To have an enduring effect, treat your employees well on a daily basis by running your organization with feeling as per the Model for Creating Champions.

How do you know if your employees are basically happy or if they need some attention? One leading motivational psychologist describes the 3 things that employees must have in order to be successful:
1) have a high positive energy
2) be calm in their approach to their jobs and
3) have fun at what they do.
Happy employees as those with *high positive energy* and who were: alert, energetic, stimulated, inspired, vigorous, enthused, challenged, team spirited, relaxed and content. *Unhappy employees,* on the other hand, possess *high negative energy* and are: nervous, fearful, anxious, angry, frustrated, upset, vengeful, bored, disinterested, annoyed and burned out.

It's time to take inventory again. How would you describe your employees? If they're unhappy, use the Creating Champions Model as well as incentive programs to boost morale, If they're happy, incentive programs will ignite them to increase productivity, to focus their attention on problem areas, to generate better ideas, to reduce costs, to increase sales and to have fun. Fast forward to the introduction of Part D. Chart #14 lists 25 major benefits of running incentive programs.

Business is often related to sports. It has been proven that golf, for example, is 1% physical and 99% mental. Think about all the sets of 18 holes in which you scored well. Weren't you at your mental best? Happy, content, relaxed. Now, think about all those balls (with your name on them) living at the bottom of the course's lake. How happy were you on those days?! In the nineties, we are entering an electronic and communications world of unforseen dimensions. It will be the most competitive decade in history. To meet the challenge, organizations today must work smarter and be more productive. Creative thinking can help you get there. Use incentive programs to inspire your troops, to fill them with high positive energies. You, too, will be happier for it...and just think about the money you'll save on unlost golf balls!

WHO DO YOU INCENTIZE?

Raise your hands. How many of you like to be patted on the back for a job well done? How many Chief Executive Officers just raised their hands? Everyone from the top of the organization to the bottom enjoys being recognized. Three things drive people: money, opportunity and recognition.

People in every conceivable position in the organization can be encouraged to improve their performance - all managers and all non-managers. Sales people are often the only employees to be incentized. I have heard grumblings down the hall of a few organizations, "How come the sales people get all the rewards and all the fun?"

All employees need to feel important and to feel a part of the team. Receptionists, shippers, customer service, secretaries, clerks, managers, CEO's, vice-presidents, marketing staff, finance and manufacturing would all enjoy some fun and recognition. And how about your dealers? Your suppliers? Use incentive programs to rouse the mind and the spirit of all these people.

Experience, by those who have run programs in the past, has taught that the most successful programs have included an incentive for the employee *and* his/her Manager. For example, a Sales Manager is really a Sales Rep with a few additional years of experience. They never stop wanting to win. They're still high achievers. They still thrive on recognition and praise. For these reasons, pump up the adrenalin of your Management team from time to time. While you are incentizing the reps, devise a program for the Managers. Watch them drive those employees to be successful!

OBJECTIVES

Once again, I'll refer you to Chart #14 in Part D for a full list of objectives. The benefits of running incentive programs can be divided into two areas: people benefits and number benefits. Let's look at some of the more common reasons for incorporating incentive plans into your business plans:

1. *People like to work in an invigorating environment.* Human beings spend the better part of their day working away from their homes. By making their workplace a warm, exciting and challenging place to work, you will be rewarded by happier employees, increased productivity, better customer service, and a stronger team who will remain loyal to the organization over the years.

2. *Cash flow is suffering and your sales for the month, quarter or year end are falling short of your goal.* Encourage the team (the entire company) to boost sales. Yes, it can be done. Even those in non-sales positions can propel your sales over the top.

3. *Profits for the month, quarter or year end are sagging.* Invite all employees to participate in a program for profits.

4. *Inventory levels and/or days outstanding in accounts receivable are too high.* Urge your people to reduce these vital stats down to an acceptable level by introducing an invigorating program.

5. *Productivity per employee is low.* Perhaps morale is low. Develop a stimulating program that will inject some fun into the workplace and improve productivity at the same time. Chances are that the results of the short-term program will boost productivity for the long term.

6. *Certain product line sales are slow.* You may have a need to encourage used equipment sales or provide a catalyst for your hardware driven salespeople to concentrate on supply sales or service agreements. Or, you have just launched a new product line and want the sales force to get excited over the new lineup. Occasionally, you may find a drop in sales of a particular type of product and your inventories are piling up. Along with discovering why the product isn't selling, create a program to incite the troops to action.

7. *Your sales or other business factors, ie; accounts receivable appear to be seasonal.* Plan to implement some of your most powerful programs, when you know that historically your sales or other business factors are not at their best. Another good idea is to implement powerful progams during a time when you know you'll reap the biggest benefit, ie: year end.

HOW LONG SHOULD YOUR PROGRAMS BE?

Choose the length of your programs to match your goals. For example, if your goal is to increase sales for the month, choose a short-term game plan. A quarterly agenda will allow the employees time to plan their individual or group modus operandi. If the task is time consuming (lowering inventories or accounts receivable, selling a particular slow-moving product), ensure that the participants have ample time in which to achieve their goals. Contests where the reward comes at the end of a year of hard work usually only recognize the cream of the crop and the experienced worker. It is, therefore, very important to remember to have a good mix of programs from short- to long-term. The new and inexperienced employees have a better chance of winning the short-term races. The long service or experienced employee will usually benefit more from the long-term programs. These employees have learned how to consistently produce results.

HOW MANY PROGRAMS SHOULD YOU BE RUNNING?

A program that runs for an entire year and where the big reward comes at the end of the year can be run at the same time as your short-term programs. The goals will be different.

A good rule of thumb is to introduce only one short-term program per category of employee at any given time. By running one at a time, you are ensuring full concentration by your employees and/or your dealers. Too many programs with different objectives will confuse the participants and dilute their efforts.

During your business planning process give careful consideration to how and when you will be running your programs. Draw up a calendar showing the annual programs and short-term programs by category of employee. Within any given category, let's take sales for example, do not run programs back-to-back on a regular basis. There should not be a program going on every month. The sales people will begin to get bored with month after month of incentive programs. Give them breaks. Give yourself a break. There is one exception to this rule. You can run a sales related and a non-sales related program back to back. For example, one month you can run "U-TOP-1A" and the next month you can run "Undercover Agent". (See index.) One is sales related and the other is awareness related with a strong team building component.

It's appropriate at this time to look at budgets. Once you've laid out your business plan, determine how much money you're going to need per employee per program at the national level. At the local level, consider budgeting $25 per month per branch employee. These dollars can be used by the Branch Manager to run his/her own local programs. Once you've run a full year of scheduled programs, you'll want to include some of the better ones in next year's plan. Since much of the ground work will have been done, your second year's programs should cost you less in terms of time and dollars.

WHO EXECUTES THE PROGRAMS?

Usually, programs executed by the employee's Manager are the most successful. The Manager then has ownership in the program and will ensure it's success. The Manager will also know which employees will need assistance in carrying out the program. He/she is responsible for motivating his/her employees on a daily basis; therefore, it makes sense that any special programs should be launched by that individual as well. Head Office Managers may create the program but the front line managers should be responsible for the execution *and* results. In the case of company-wide programs, endorsement by the CEO in the form of a memo or video message adds extra weight to the program.

For many programs, I've also sent packages to the employees' homes. The power of the spouse to motivate cannot be underestimated. The family then joins this awesome team in achieving results. Choose prizes which will grace anyone's home or which the entire family can enjoy (restaurant dinners, tickets to special events, etc.).

The launch of incentive programs *must be* an exciting event. Teach your Managers how to sell Hype. Their launch packages should contain everything they need:
- visual overheads explaining the entire program
- sample of prizes
- support materials (posters, buttons, video, noise makers, flags, key chains, etc.).

At the end of the presentation, you should be able to peel the employees off of the ceiling! Hype sells.

MEASUREMENT

Where possible, the success of each motivational program should be measured. Set realistic goals at the beginning of each program and then measure the results at the end. In the case of a year long agenda, take a cursory glance at the results every quarter to ensure the program is on track. Are you meeting your objectives? Are the participants still active in the program? Occasionally, year long programs may need to be revised if participation starts to drop. Long-term programs need to be continually advertised to the troops. Short, surprise bursts of enthusiasm through an additional bonus point can keep the participants motivated to reach their goals. See index for "Double Your Earnings! Double Your Fun!"

Measurement of the results will tell you the level of success of the program and if changes need to be made to improve upon the results. Successful plans received with enthusiasm will be asked for again, year after year. Your staff will look forward to them and develop a competitive spirit months before you even launch the incentive.

PLANNING

Earlier, we discussed the importance of drawing up an incentive calendar as part of your organization's business plan. Prior to your casting the plan in concrete, it's a good idea to involve your Managers in the thinking process. At one of your Management meetings, be it with Head Office or Field Managers or both, ask them for assistance. These people are the ones closest to the street fighters and should be a good resource of ideas. In addition, once you have released the programs to the employees, the Managers will have a sense of ownership in their creation. The implementation will be done quickly and with greater enthusiasm. The Managers also need to be ''sold'' on the idea or the results will not be as good as they could have been.

PRIZES

There are scads of ideas for prizes. Cash, merchandise, travel, gift certificates and wacky prizes are all highly sought-after items. The following list is a drop in the bucket of ideas from heaven. They range from low to high cost:

T-shirts/sweat shirts	encyclopedia
cook books	toaster
plaques	microwave
recognition certificates	china
cash	crystal
gift baskets	jewellery
pens/mechanical pencils with co. logo	cutlery
portfolios with names gold stamped	silverware
briefcases	glassware
watches	figurines/sculptures
cameras	limited edition prints
video cameras	original works of art
VCR's	dinners for two
disk players	tickets to special events
gift certificates to restaurants and stores	sports equipment
TV's	auto tires
cellular phones	win your weight in gold
personal fax	silver dollars
personal computers	pay all your bills
portable phones	limo for the weekend
paid income tax	two servants for a day
new car/Jeep	shares in the company
a day at a spa	African safari (or any travel)
pay off all debts	shopping spree
tool kits	water skis
sailing boat	snow skis
magazine subscriptions	

Choose your prizes carefully. Prizes need not be expensive. In fact, experience shows that simple rewards are just as effective. Twenty-year veterans as well as junior employees are happy to receive a plaque. The recognition is what they're after. A plaque, a certificate, a handshake or the winner's name on a cake presented at a meeting is often all that is required. Having said that, a steady stream of plaques can get a little boring. Vary the prizes from program to program. Ensure that your prizes will be attractive to the majority of recipients. The latest electronic gadgets are always a big hit. Merchandise catalogues are fun to browse through for more ideas.

THE AWARDS CELEBRATION

The most important part of any incentive program is the Awards Celebration. Remember that there are two things that people want more than sex and money — recognition and praise (this according to Mary Kay Ash). Whatever the prize, put your star in the limelight for a length of time. Let them bask in the glory of their success. Make the recognition a celebration — pretend that it's the Academy Awards! At annual conventions, recognize high achievers in front of their peers. At other times, gather the employees together. In small organizations, invite all employees to witness the recognition even if it's a sales-only program. The other employees will have helped the individual win and they will want to praise him or her as well. As the Manager, have a speech prepared to praise the individual(s) for his or her work as you invite the employee to come to the front of the room. Provide the group with details and results. Then ask the employee(s) to share with everyone what special things he or she did to go over the top. It'll turn into a learning experience for everyone.

Special gatherings like lunch meets are fun. Everyone can bring their own lunch and the company can provide dessert — a cake with the individual's name written in icing. Or, if the prize is a substantial one, honor your hero at a wine and cheese party, to which spouses and friends have been invited.

Whatever the prize, whenever the ceremony, remember to recognize and praise the high achievers — make them feel like royalty.

LEGALITIES

It's wise to check with the appropriate authorities for rules and regulations concerning contests run in the geographic area you have chosen. Your advertising or promotional company can assist you. For internally run contests where no consumer is involved, chances are that you won't have to register anywhere. Once the consumer is involved, you may be required to register with the Post

Office, the Federal Trade Commission and the Federal Communications Commission in the U.S. In Canada, contests open to anyone where no purchases are required must follow the rules of the Competition Act. You will be obliged to disclose the value of the prize and the draw date and include a skill testing question among other items. If a purchase is required in order to enter, you are now running a lottery and need to contact the three U.S. federal agencies above. In Canada, the provincial lottery commission needs to know about your program and they'll probably issue a license and register your program. Quebec has their own set of rules. Contact the Régie des loteries et courses du Québec for details. Don't let the federal/provincial/state regulatory bodies bog you down. It's not as tough as it seems.

One more point with respect to legalities. Any prize that is won must be declared as taxable income. The participants should know this up front.

DESIGNING YOUR OWN PROGRAMS

The programs in Parts C, D and E of this book should keep you going for a while. However, should you wish to design your own, simply follow the template of the programs in this book. Define the program's objectives. From there, describe the participants, the length of the program, the details including rules, prizes, support materials, agendas and costs. Include how you're going to measure the results of the program and what changes you'd make for next year. Lastly, describe the recognition and praise process. Good luck!

THE 3 R's OF BUSINESS

RISK - REWARD - RECOGNITION. Employees take a risk joining any organization. For some, the risk is higher if they are non-salaried or on commission. Every employee enjoys receiving a reward for work accomplished. Along with the reward comes the recognition in front of their peers. The recognition makes the risk all worthwhile.

SUMMARY

"Sales are up 30%! Productivity has improved! Our profits have soared!" Incentive programs really do work. In my experience, programs that I've run had been most effective in reaching our objectives. The effort put in to them was appreciated by all employees. I'll never forget one year end program where we had everyone in the company involved. Our sales had slipped over the course of the year and we were several million dollars short of our annual forecast. The goal seemed unreachable. The program not only put us over our sales target but bettered our profits by a couple percentage points! The lesson we learned was this:

IN A CRISIS, DON'T BE AFRAID TO ASK ALL OF YOUR EMPLOYEES TO HELP YOU REACH YOUR SALES AND PROFIT TARGETS. YOU'LL BE AMAZED AT THE TEAMWORK AND THE RESULTS.

Motivated employees, Champion employees, are worth their weight in gold. Treat them as such.

PART C:

4 MAGICAL ANNUAL INCENTIVE PROGRAMS

4 MAGICAL ANNUAL INCENTIVE PROGRAMS

In North America alone, companies spend billions of dollars on trade incentives every year. Roughly 25% of those dollars are spent on travel. The magic of travel.

Travel incentives are great motivators. A year of hard work pays off in a few glorious days in the sun. What drives these people to win?

- The pride of achieving a stretch quota.
- "I've done it." The pride of saying to your spouse/companion, "Honey, we're going on a *free* holiday."
- The pride of joining your professional peers for a week of comradeship.
- The pride of knowing that you're good at what you do.
- The pride of being recognized by senior management as a top achiever.
- A week away from the kids!
- The joy of relaxing in the sun!

Yes, travel is a powerful motivator. "Dream Trippers" in this section will help you plan that magical holiday.

There are numerous other annual programs that can be run. "The 100% Club", for example, recognizes your top achievers through pins, rings, plaques, etc.. I have watched this program work well for new sales recruits as well as for seasoned reps. Long-term incentive programs such as these provide your people with long-term goals - something to reach for. Short-term programs can give you short bursts of high productivity. It's the long-term ones that demand *consistency of performance*.

LONG-TERM INCENTIVE PROGRAMS COMMAND CONSISTENCY IN EMPLOYEE PERFORMANCE.

One of the toughest jobs that a sales corporation has is keeping its Dealers motivated to sell their products when Dealers carry multiple brands and several product lines. I've created "Star Reach - A Dealer Program" as an annual incentive tool to:

1) Encourage Dealers to sell your products versus other brands on the shelf.

2) Develop a "family" feeling between the Dealers themselves and between the Dealers and Head Office.

3) Discourage Dealers from leaving the fold.

4) Recognize the achievements of large *and small* Dealers.

5) Recognize the hard work of *the staff* at the top dealerships.

6) Build your company's reputation as one that wins dealer loyalty. Other dealers will be knocking on your door to carry your product lines.

Last, but not least of the 4 magical incentive programs, is "Star Reach - The Newsletter." Everyone loves to see their name in print. The Newsletter does three things:

1) It recognizes the achievements of your company's "stars", on a monthly basis.

2) It communicates the year-to-date standings of everyone for the annual incentive programs such as "Dream Trippers" and "The 100% Club".

3) It brings the country together. Thousands of miles of activity is printed in one small newsletter. Joe in Virginia can see how his training buddy in Seattle is doing. Will they see each other in Hawaii on a Dream Trip? Watch them spur each other on.

Long-term incentives are catalysts for success. Use them to encourage consistency in performance.

The 100% Club

- Only the very best Sales Representatives achieve membership in the 100% club.

- The awards distinguish individuals for being among the few who have risen to professional sales excellence.

Company Logo

THE 100% CLUB

DESCRIPTION   This superlative program runs all year long and is the type that is used by many companies as their premier recognition program. Employees receive pins, plaques and 10K gold rings for 100+ points in selling units of product. The rings are heavily sought after items. They will be worn with pride.

PARTICIPANTS   Field Sales Reps in Branch and Dealer offices.

OTHER APPLICATIONS: The program's objectives and rules can be modified to suit:
1) Government Employees, Administrators, Plant Workers, Telemarketing Reps and Customer Support Employees: reward the best ideas for improving productivity, reducing costs and/or increasing profits. Increase your telephone sales, reduce receivables, accelerate billings, reduce manufacturing waste.

2) Service Technicians: reward an increase in the number of calls they make in a day, improve the quality of service, increase the sale of service contracts and lower-priced products (supplies, accessories, etc.).

3) All Employees: create or maintain a happy working environment. Generate ideas for increasing productivity, reducing costs and/or increasing profits.

This program can be run locally, regionally or nationally.

OBJECTIVES   1) To recognize your top performers. Target for 35% of the field force to become members of the 100% club.

2) To encourage sales of high-end, high-ticket items.

LENGTH   12 months.

DETAILS   The "Rules" for the 100% Club appear in the ensuing pages.

The goal of the Sales Rep is to reach a minimum of 100 points at the end of the year. See the page entitled "100% Club Awards" for details of levels of achievement.

Sourcing of the awards can be done through many types of suppliers. It's wise to keep a supply of certificates, plaques and pins on hand in the event that a few of your go-getter reps achieve 100 points before the year is up. Hand them out as soon as possible. Instant recognition works best.

Setting the point values for your products must be done with care. Take a look at last year's sales of 35% of your top sales people. That's how many you will want to win this year. Study the units sold. Assign point values to each of the products they sold until 20% of them would have made 100 points, 10% would have made 125 points and 5% would have made over 125 points. The more expensive your product, the more points they will receive. See the page entitled "Point Values".

If you have several product lines sold by separate sales forces, create point value charts for each product line.

Support materials for the field can be as follows:

1) A booklet contains the rules, the point values and details of the awards. Pictures of the awards would be an asset. Include an example copy of a complete Sales Monthly Summary report showing the point values earned.

2) A set of overhead visuals which the Branch Manager/Dealer Owner can use to launch the program and re-use for new recruits.

3) A poster hung in each sales room will frequently remind them of the program.

MEASUREMENT   Determine the number of awards presented for the program. Did you reach your goal — 35% of the sales force achieved 100+ points?

Has the program helped to encourage the sale of high ticket items?

Determine the participation level by dealer rep and branch rep.

Determine the excitement level. Were most people interested?

Determine the cost of the program as a % of sales.

Recommend changes, if any, to future programs.

RECOGNITION   With year-long programs, it's important to keep the momentum going.

Have the 100% Club Coordinator send out reminders every once in a while on what the awards are all about.

Every quarter, send the personalized certificates out as quickly as possible to reinforce the achievement. The Branch

Manager/Dealer Owner should present the certificates at the next weekly sales meeting. Let the rep bask in the victor's circle for awhile. Applaud the achievement. Take him/her out for lunch.

At the local meetings, train the Branch Manager/Dealer Owners to applaud everyone's hard work. Make everyone feel like a winner while heaping special praise upon your star performers.

The pins, pendants and plaques are to be presented as soon as the achievement level has been reached. Each ring, the pièce de résistance, should be presented at an event where your superstars can be recognized in front of a large group of their peers.

A congratulatory memo from the National Sales Manager and the President/CEO should be sent to each 100% Club member.

100% CLUB AWARDS

ACHIEVEMENT	AWARD	TIME OF PRESENTATION
• 25 points in any quarter of the year	100% Club Certificate	Immediately
• 100 points. First time achievers	• 100% Club embossed 10k gold lapel pin or pendant	Immediately
	• 100% Club embossed 10k gold ring with a semi precious stone (emeralds, rubies, onyx, etc.)	At a convention if possible
• 100-125 points	• Bronze plaque with name engraved	Immediately
• 126-150 points	• Silver plaque with name engraved	Immediately
• 150+ points	• Gold plaque with name engraved •100% Club gold pen	Immediately
• Every year that a rep receives 125+ points	• A diamond is added to his/her ring	If possible, this presentation should be made at a convention where these superstars can be recognized in front of a large group of peers

100% CLUB

- POINT VALUES -

PRODUCT TYPE	RETAIL VALUE OF NEW SALE	TYPE OF SALE	POINT VALUE
PRODUCT A	$50,000	New Sale*	7
		Used	5
		Rental	4
PRODUCT B	$40,000	New Sale	6
		Used	4
		Rental	3
PRODUCT C	$30,000	New Sale	5
		Used	3
		Rental	2
PRODUCT D	$20,000	New Sale	4
		Used	2
		Rental	1
PRODUCT E	$10,000	New Sale	3
		Used	1
		Rental	.5

* Sale or Lease

NOTE: The higher the retail value of the product, the greater the point value in all types of sale: new, used or rental.

THE 100% CLUB

— RULES —

1. The 100% Club is open to all Sales Representatives in Branch offices and authorized Dealer locations.

2. The 100% Club year runs January 1st. through December 31st.

3. Point values are earned in the month in which a system is installed in a customer's office.

4. In the event that a product is sold in one territory and installed in another territory, each rep will receive 50% of the point value of the system.

5. Point values will be lost if a product is returned from a customer's office.

6. Sales Representatives transferred from one product line to another will carry their points with them and continue building points with their new product line.

7. The point values earned are to be recorded on a Sales Monthly Summary for each rep. Sales Monthly Summaries are to be received by the 100% Club Coordinator by the 5th working day of each month. From time to time, Dealer Reps may be asked to submit copies of invoices as proof of sale.

8. In clarification of terms, a rental contract is a system placed on a firm 12 month or more contract whereas a new sale is a product that has never previously been sold.

9. The certificates, pins, pendants, plaques and pens will be awarded immediately upon reaching the appropriate achievement level. The rings will be presented at the annual convention.

10. 100% Club values are subject to change by Senior Management at any time.

11. All questions involving interpretation of these rules should be addressed to the 100% Club Coordinator.

Company Logo

DREAM TRIPPERS

Aim high and enjoy a magical week of sun and surf and fun! . . . Achieve sales excellence, join the best of the best and become a dream tripper.

Company Logo

DREAM TRIPPERS

DESCRIPTION   Everybody loves a holiday! Challenge your people to "aim high". Upon achieving peak sales performance, the Dream Trippers will enjoy membership in an exclusive club. A magical week at an exotic location - all expenses paid - awaits their arrival.

PARTICIPANTS   Field Sales Reps in Branch and Dealer offices, Dealer Owners, Branch Managers, Sales Managers, National Sales Managers, National Marketing Managers.

OTHER APPLICATIONS: The program's objectives and rules can be modified to suit:

1) Government Employees, Administrators, Plant Workers, Telemarketing Reps and Customer Support Employees: reward the best ideas for improving productivity, reducing costs and/or increasing profits. Increase your telephone sales, reduce receivables, accelerate billings, reduce manufacturing waste.

2) Service Technicians: reward an increase in the number of calls they make in a day, improve the quality of service, increase the sale of service contracts and lower-priced products (supplies, accessories, etc.).

3) All Employees: create or maintain a happy working environment. Generate ideas for increasing productivity, reducing costs and/or increasing profits.

This program can be run locally, regionally or nationally.

OBJECTIVES   1. To reward outstanding sales achievement. 60-70% of your field force should make trip.

2. To improve sales over last year.

3. Your top performers will love the chance to meet their peers and discuss problems/opportunities (good for future business).

4. To build a stronger field sales team.

5. Senior Managers can schedule meetings during the trip to keep the field force informed of the company's progress and to keep them pumped for the next year's sales.

LENGTH

12 months. Run the contest January 1st. through December 31st. The Dream Trip should take place in March, April or May if you choose a tropical climate or earlier if you choose a skiing holiday.

DETAILS

The basic "Contest Rules" appear on the following pages. They can be modified to suit your organization's requirements.

Setting the trip quotas is the toughest job of all. They *must* be fair. Some company's choose to have only 10-15% of their field force earn Dream Trip. That means that the majority of the sales force feels like losers. The most motivating trips are ones where the trip quotas are indeed a stretch yet 60-70% of the field force physically make the trip.

The fairest method of setting quotas is to look at each individual's achievement for the last year and study the potential in their territory. For more details see the page located towards the end of this program entitled "Dream Trip - Various Methods of Setting Quotas".

The trip is open to all sales employees/dealers and a guest. The guest could be a spouse or adult friend or relative. Some companies choose to pay for all expenses of the Dream Tripper's guest. Others offer to pay a certain percentage of the expenses based upon the percent attainment of trip quota by the winner. Having worked both scenarios, I suggest that the former is the preferred approach. If a winner has hustled his/her behind for a whole year, you can bet your boots that the spouse has eagerly supported the idea. They both deserve to "win". (Since Dealers own their own companies, it is not uncommon to ask the Dealers to share in the cost of the program for their own reps.)

Choosing the location is fun. In my experience, most companies choose either a tropical or European location. Sun and sand seem to be synonymous with fun! On the other hand, I've been on Dream Trips only a thousand or two miles away from home and had a great time. Reserve well in advance. If the group is large with 500+ people, you'll need a resort that specializes in handling groups of this size.

THE LAUNCH

The launch and follow-through of Dream Trip must be thought out carefully. Launch it with posters and a video of the dream vacation spot. Every month send a reminder *to the participants' homes.* The spouses will then add encouragement to make sales. There are scads of ideas to use for the follow-through. The reminders could be bags of sand, sunglasses, plastic tropical-looking glasses, bath foam, postcards mailed from your trip location, etc. Keep them pumped and keep them informed of their progress by publishing a monthly newsletter. See "Star Reach - The Newsletter".

In the launch kit, include Sales Charts for the Sales Reps, Sales Managers and Dealer Owners. Every day or week they can clock their progress towards Dream Trip. On one part of the Dealer Owner chart, bullet list all the benefits of being a 3-4-5 star Dealer (see Star Reach - a Dealer Program). Also bullet list the benefits of being the top dealer in each category. The individuals will then team up to help each other win. The reps will want their Branch Managers or Dealer Owners to win as well. Great teamwork.

THE AGENDA

Plan the agenda to include some business (for tax purposes and for communicating to your people), lots of pleasure, special spouse programs, group sporting and sightseeing activities and, of course, an awards banquet for the Dream Trippers Club members.

A suggested "Agenda" follows. Here are a few tips for that agenda:
- Organize the arrival to run like clockwork. Hand out arrival packages containing agendas, T-shirts, beach bags, etc. Before dinner, coordinate a Welcome Cocktail Party. On the first official morning, gather the club members and their spouses/guests for a meeting. This, in my mind, is the most important part of the entire trip. Use this meeting to build teamwork and respect for upper management. The most powerful agenda that I've witnessed has been one where Senior Management treats the club members as valued employees. (I have also been involved in situations where this was not the case.) Give them the true picture about the company's position in terms of sales and profits. If the

position isn't so good, Senior Managers should ask the members for help in improving the numbers. Talk to them about all the successes and all the failures. If a product has problems, the field force sure knows it. Tell them what you're going to do about it. Treat the members as professionals and they will reward *you* with professional results. Equally important, recognize the spouses for their support.

- On the second day prior to the main Awards Banquet have a special reception for all winners and guests who have been with the company over 10 years. Recognize the loyalty.

- The Awards Banquet should be a sumptuous affair - a sit down dinner with wine. Afterwards, keep the Awards Ceremony short. I've been on trips where every trip winner received a plaque and a photo with the Prez. If you've got several hundred winners, the night goes on forever.

The best Awards Ceremony I've seen consists of only 2 Sales Rep awards given per region. One goes to the top ranking rep and the second to the runner-up. All remaining reps and managers were simply happy to have won the trip.

To recognize all winners in some way, you can do many things:

1. Publish all winners names in a pre-trip newsletter.
2. At the banquet, every winner's name can appear on slides on two screens at the front of the room. One name per slide will fill them with pride.
3. Present each member with a lapel pin sometime during the week.

- Hire a good band.

- Give special recognition throughout the week to the spouses who have encouraged the hard work ethic. I had one Sales Manager who didn't dare go home with zero sales for any day throughout the year. His wife clocked his progress because she was definitely going on a trip. Talk about pressure!

- I know of one company that knows how to make its people feel first rate. Every year the Simplex International Time Equipment Co. hires a top entertainer for the evening. Barbara Mandrell, Smokey Robinson, Jay Leno and Crystal Gayle have all entertained the Simplex 100% Club at various exotic resorts. Now, wouldn't you be thinking ''Gee, they think we're so important that they've hired a top entertainer just for us!''? Chris Watkins, the President of this same company always receives a standing ovation when he approaches the podium. He expects the best from his people and rewards them for their achievements.

- Bring in one-hour motivational speakers to talk on everything from inspiring people to be self-motivated (ie. their employees), to recruiting and training.
- Consider organizing a spur-of-the-moment talent show. You'll be amazed at the talent in the room!

MEASUREMENT   Determine what % of the sales force made trip. Did it meet your target? If not, ask yourself why not.

Determine the overall sales increase of Dream Trippers this year over last year.

Determine the true participation level by all. Were they keen?

Look at the overall costs of the program as a percent of sales.

Recommend changes, if any, to future programs.

RECOGNITION   Most of this area was covered in the section under the Awards Banquet. Whatever you do, organize the Awards with care. It is the recognition night of the year. Make it special for everyone. I know of many horror stories. During the Awards Banquet of company A, the Canadians were not allowed to receive their awards at the podium alongside their American counterparts. They were forced to have a separate ceremony at 11 o'clock that evening in the hallway. In addition, the band played only the American anthem when the room had other countries represented. Know your audience to ensure that everyone is treated equally.

At the time when you are announcing the Dream Trip winners to the field, have the National Sales Manager and President/CEO send a letter of recognition or telegram to each and every winner. Sending a rose would also be a nice touch. Send it to their homes so that the spouses can share in the excitement.

NOTES   This program, as designed, is targeted at sales people. You might think about creating a spot for a non-sales type. This person, who would go as your guest, might be a non-sales executive or any other type of employee who has done an extraordinary job over the past year.

The detail work required to organize a trip incentive program is awesome. It's wise to enlist the services of a professional trip incentive company. They usually have the organization of such trips down to a fine art.

"DREAM TRIP"
— AGENDA —

SATURDAY

All Day ....Arrivals

6:30 p.m...Reception - ALL (Casual)
Grand Ballroom Foyer

7:30 p.m. ....Dinner - ALL (Casual)
(give location)

SUNDAY

7:30 - 9:00 a.m. ....Breakfast - ALL (Casual)
(give location)

9:30 a.m. ....Opening Meeting - ALL (Casual)
Grand Ballroom

11:45 a.m. - 1:15 p.m..Lunch (Casual)
(give location)

Noon - 6:00 p.m., ...Activities, Free Time

6:00 - 7:00 p.m., ...10 Year Club Reception (Business)
(give location)

6:30 - 7:30 p.m. ....Reception (Business)
(give location)

7:30 p.m. ....Awards Banquet
(Business)
Grand Ballroom

10:00 p.m. - Midnight ....Dancing
Grand Ballroom

MONDAY

7:00 - 8:00 a.m...................................Breakfast - Meeting Attendees **Only**
(Casual)

7:45 - 8:45 a.m., ...Branch Managers (Casual)
(give location)

8:00 - 9:00 a.m. ....Breakfast - Spouses **Only** (Casual)
(give location)

9:00 - 11:30 a.m. ....Product X Session (Casual)
(give location)
9:00 - 11:30 a.m. ....Product Y Session (Casual)
(give location)
9:00 a.m. - Noon ....Spouse Program - Craft Fair (Casual)
(give location)
Noon - 1:30 p.m. ....Lunch (Casual)
(give location)
Noon - 6:00 p.m. ....Activities, Free Time
7:00 p.m. ....Dinner (Casual)
(give location)

TUESDAY

7:00 - 8:00 a.m. ....Breakfast - Meeting Attendees **Only** (Casual)
(give location)
8:00 - 9:00 a.m. ....Breakfast - Spouses **not** attending
Fashion Show (Casual)
(give location)
8:00 - 11:00 a.m. ....Breakfast/Fashion Show (Casual)
Spouses per sign-up
(give location)
8:15 - 9:45 a.m. ....Region Breakouts
• NC Region - (give location)
• NE Region - (give location)
• SE Region - (give location)
• WE Region - (give location)
• CE Region - (give location)
• Canada   - (give location)
9:45 - 10:05 a.m. ....Break - Grand Ballroom Foyer
10:10 - 11:30 a.m. ....General Meeting - Meeting Attendees (Casual)
Grand Ballroom
Noon - 1:30 p.m. ....Lunch (Casual)
(give location)
Noon - 6:00 p.m. ....Activities, Free Time
6:30 - 8:30 p.m. ....Dinner (Casual)
(give location)
9:00 p.m. ....Special Entertainment - ALL (Casual)
Grand Ballroom

WEDNESDAY

7:00 - 8:30 a.m......................Breakfast - Meeting Attendees **Only** (Casual)
(give location)
8:00 - 9:30 a.m. ....Breakfast - Spouses (Casual)
(give location)
8:45 - 9:45 a.m....................General Meeting (Casual) - Meeting Attendees
(give location)
9:45 - 10:00 a.m..Break - Grand Ballroom Foyer
10:05 - 11:30 a.m......................General Meeting - Guest Speaker (Casual)
Meeting Attendees and Spouses invited
Grand Ballroom
Noon - 1:30 p.m..Lunch (Casual)
Noon. - 6:00 p.m. ....Activities, Free Time
6:30 - 7:15 p.m. ....Reception - ALL (Casual)
(give location)
7:15 p.m. ....Farewell Dinner - ALL (Casual)
Grand Ballroom
9:45 - 11:30 p.m. ....Dancing - ALL Grand Ballroom

THURSDAY

5:30 - 6:30 a.m..Continental Breakfast,
Early Departures
(give location)
6:30 - 8:30 a.m. ....Breakfast, Grand Ballroom
ALL DAY..Departures

NOTES:

1. Locations for functions shown In (   ) indicate where event will be
   held in case of rain, etc.
2. Dress:
   Casual................Men - sport shirt, dress slacks; Women - skirt, slacks
   Business...............................Men - suit, tie; Women - suit, dress, skirt
   Recreational ......shorts, t-shirts, etc. - Appropriate for selected activities

DREAM TRIP

— Various Methods of Setting Quotas —

SALES REPS

1. Look at each individual's total sales numbers for last year. Study the territorial potential and set quota.

or

2. Divide this group into two: those with less than a year of sales experience and those with more than a year. The former would have a lower quota.

or

3. Divide this group into categories of tenure. The sales results are weighted as follows:

   Category A: Reps $\geq$ 2 years experience = \$ Sales x 1.00% = contest \$ submitted

   Category B: Reps $\geq$ 1 year and < 2 years experience = \$ Sales x 1.25% contest \$ submitted

   Category C: Reps < 1 year experience = \$ Sales x 1.50% contest \$ submitted.

   Weighting allows all reps the opportunity by giving the junior reps a bit of a head start over the more experienced reps who should find the selling game a lot easier.

SALES MANAGERS

1. Look at each individual's sales numbers for the last year, study the territorial potential and take into account the number of Sales Reps under his/her wing and set quota.

2. You can set the Sales Manager's quotas based on hardware sales only or on all sales in the territory.

BRANCH MANAGERS/MANAGERS OF DEALER TERRITORIES

1. In most cases, you will already have set a general annual sales forecast for this group. It should be based on sales *and* profits. If the sales forecast is a stretch from last year, there's no need to add more stretch.

2. Another method of setting quotas is to work this group as a team. For example, if the company attains less than 100% of their sales and profit target, one Manager with the highest % over his/her forecast will win Dream Trip.

   DIVISION ATTAINMENT $\geq$ 100% but $\leq$ 101%
   2 highest Managers over forecast win

   DIVISION ATTAINMENT $\geq$ 101% but $\leq$ 102%
   3 highest Managers over forecast win

   and so on.

NATIONAL SALES MANAGERS AND NATIONAL MARKETING MANAGERS

Company-wide attainment of the sales and profit goals for the year will earn this group a place in the sun.

GUEST

There may be one person that you select to attend trip as the co's guest. It could be a non-sales executive or an employee who has exhibited outstanding performance during the year.

DREAM TRIP

— CONTEST RULES —

GENERAL

1. This contest is open to all company Sales Reps, authorized Dealer Sales Reps, authorized Dealer Owners, Branch Managers, Sales Managers and National Sales and Marketing Managers.

2. All Club Members may bring either their spouse or an adult guest of their choice. Guest must be over 18 years of age.

3. Contest quotas are as per the Quota Sheet.

4. Any new participant hired with less than eight months remaining in the contest period must attain a minimum of eight months equivalent of contest quota in order to qualify.

5. Sales credits generated for sales which were made during the contest year will be charged against both the current contest year's quota attainment and next year's attainment.

6. Any Manager whose trip quota is based on sales and profits must make their target in both areas.

   If the quota forecasts a loss in profit for the contest year, the Manager must either meet or better their target for the contest year in order to qualify for Dream Trip. Trip quota is based on total revenue dollars.

7. Sales reinstated after the close of business for this contest year cannot be credited to this year's contest quota. These reinstatements will be credited to next year's contest sales.

8. All sales which qualify a participant for Dream Trip must be paid for prior to the trip; lease payments must be current at the time of the trip. If sales or leases do not meet these conditions, year-to-date trip quota attainment for the trip contest will be reduced accordingly.

9. In order to be counted, sales made prior to the end of the contest year must be delivered, installed and billed prior to close of the contest period.

10. As required by government regulations, the Dream Trip for winner and spouse attendees is considered taxable income.

11. Contest trip rules as stated are not subject to modification. Any questions regarding interpretation of these rules are to be addressed to the President and C.E.O.

TRANSFERS/PROMOTIONS/TERMINATIONS

1. Newly hired participants will be assigned a quota as per the quota schedule. The first contest month shall be determined in accordance with the following schedule (example hire dates given):

HIRE DATE	FIRST CONTEST MONTH
December 5 - December 20	January
January 2 - January 26	February
January 29 - February 23	March
February 26 - March 30	April
April 2 - April 27	May
April 30 - May 25	June
May 28 - June 29	July
July 2 - July 27	August
July 30 - August 24	September
August 27 - September 28	October
October 1 - October 26	November
October 24 - November 23	December

2. Anyone transferred from one category to another during the contest year, will take with them full credit for their year-to-date quota attainment. Example: If you are 95% of year-to-date quota in your previous position and your new year-to-date quota is $100,000, your new year-to-date dollar volume starting in your new position will be $95,000 (95% of 100,000). This amount will be used from that point on to determine your percentage of trip quota attainment.

3. If a Sales Rep or Sales Manager transfers to a position not eligible for Dream Trip, full credit will be given for the sales made during the months that he or she was eligible for the contest. A quota will not be assigned for the months that he or she is in a position ineligible for the contest.

4. If a Sales Rep is promoted to Sales Manager in the last four months of the contest period, he or she can qualify for Dream Trip only as a Sales Rep.

5. A. If a Sales Rep or Sales Manager is promoted to Branch Manager with six months or more remaining in the contest year, he or she will take on the year-to-date performance of that Branch and compete thereafter in the Branch Manager category.

   B. If a Sales Rep or Sales Manager is promoted to Branch Manager with less than 6 months remaining in the contest year, he or she will continue to compete as a Sales Representative or Sales Manager.

6. If a Branch Manager is transferred to a Sales Manager's or a Sales Rep's position, he or she will receive no credit for his or her performance as a Branch Manager. He or she will start the contest year at the time he or she transfers to the new position.

7. A Club Achiever who terminates his/her employment with the company or is on a leave of absence at time of the trip will be deemed ineligible to attend the trip. All trip attendees must be active employees or be part of an Authorized Dealership at the time of the trip.

8. A contest participant placed on inactive employment status because of leave of absence, will not be assigned a trip quota and will not receive credit for sales during that time period. A minimum of eight months trip quota during the remainder of the contest period is required in order to qualify for Dream Trip.

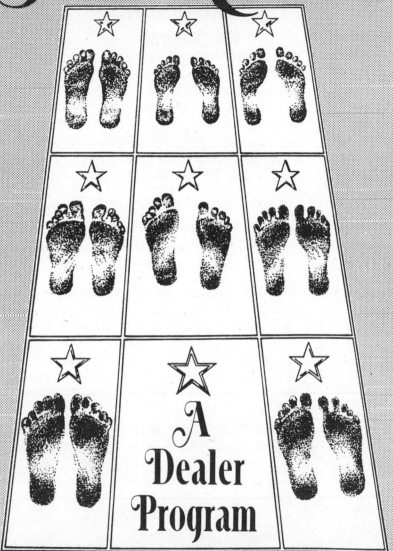

Star Reach

A Dealer Program

★ Increase your profit margins ★ Benefit from increased advertising $ ★ Be inducted onto "The Wall of Fame" ★ Take off on a VIP trip for two ★ Receive a free direct mail program ★ Treat your staff to a catered-in office party ★ and more!

Reach for the Stars!

Company Logo

STAR REACH

— A DEALER PROGRAM —

DESCRIPTION Star Reach is specifically designed to create loyalty and foster goodwill between a company and its dealer network. It is a recognition program that will make your dealers, distributors or agents proud to be part of your organization. Your top dealers will be inducted onto "The Wall of Fame". This program segments your dealer network into 3 distinct levels, based on sales volume. Each level is chock-full of rewards and recognition for a job well done yet provides motivation to aspire to a higher level.

PARTICIPANTS Dealer Owners and sales, service and administrative staff within the Dealership.

OTHER APPLICATIONS Program objectives and rules can be modified to motivate your own organization's employees as well:

1) Government Employees, Administrators, Plant Workers, Telemarketing Reps and Customer Support Employees: reward the best ideas for improving productivity, reducing costs and/or increasing profits. Increase your telephone sales, reduce receivables, accelerate billings, reduce manufacturing waste.

2) Service Technicians: reward an increase in the number of calls they make in a day, improve the quality of service, increase the sale of service contracts and lower-priced products (supplies, accessories, etc.).

3) All Employees: create or maintain a happy working environment. Generate ideas for increasing productivity, reducing costs and/or increasing profits.

4) Managers: improve productivity or sales per employee, create comraderie (a team) through friendly competition between managers.

This program can be run locally, regionally or nationally.

OBJECTIVES 1. Most Dealers will carry many products. In some cases where there is no exclusive product arrangement, Dealers can sell several brands of the same product. Star Reach will assist you in building a loyalty to your product line and your company from your Dealers *and their employees*. This loyalty should, in turn, generate more sales for your product(s). At the same time, you will build your reputation in the Dealer community. Star Reach beams a powerful message to the Dealers telling them that they are valued customers, that they are "family".

2. A good solid reputation with established Dealers will result in other new, quality Dealers banging down your door.

3. Star Reach will motivate all Dealers to sell beyond their normal sales volumes.

4. Star Reach recognizes the achievement of Dealers at all levels. We often only recognize the Dealers who sell the highest number of dollars when small Dealers may one day be your largest.

5. Star Reach also recognizes the performance of the staff at each Dealership.

LENGTH   12 months.

DETAILS   The attached sheets entitled "Star Reach Awards" detail the awards program. There are rewards for the:
1. Dealer Owner
2. New Dealers to each category
3. Top Dealers (highest sales) in each category
4. Sales Reps
5. Service Techs
6. Administrators

STAR REACH AWARDS
— DEALER OWNER —

ANNUAL SALES VOLUME	★★★ ≥ $100,000 and ≤ $200,000	★★★★ > $200,000 and ≤ $500,000	★★★★★ > $500,000
NEW DEALER	★ 3 star gold plaque embossed with dealership's name	★ 4 star gold plaque embossed with dealership's name	★ 5 star gold plaque embossed with dealership's name

— For all categories, picture in local paper with VIP from Head Office
— For all categories, billboard recognition in Dealer's market

	★★★	★★★★	★★★★★
DEALER OWNER	★ increase in profit margin with a sales volume rebate of X% ★ co-operative advertising budget at X% of sales	★ increase in profit margin with a sales volume rebate of X + 1% ★ co-operative advertising budget at X + 2% of sales	★ increase in profit margin with a sales volume rebate of X+ 2% ★ co-operative advertising budget at X + 4% of sales

— Prize catalogue gifts for all categories. Bonus points are given for each $ in sales over the minimum entry dollar volume to the star category

	★★★	★★★★	★★★★★
TOP DEALER IN EACH CATEGORY	★ additional 1% sales volume rebate ★ free direct mail campaign up to $X	★ additional 2% sales volume rebate ★ free direct mail campaign up to $X+	★ additional 3% sales volume rebate ★ free direct mail campaign up to $X++

— For all categories, picture in local newspaper with a VIP from Head Office. Arrange the feature story.
— For all categories, membership to "Wall of Fame". Wall is devoted to pictures of the TOP DEALERS with the largest sales volumes in each category. The "Wall of Fame" is located at Head Office. Dealership gets a copy of the photo.
— For all categories, free VIP trip to your Annual Convention. Large hotel suite, dinner in their honour, limo service from airport with champagne.
— For all categories, free VIP trip for two to Annual Incentive Trip, ie; Hawaii, Acapulco, etc.
— For all categories, a catered-in office party, for recognition of all the Dealerships' employees.

STAR REACH AWARDS

— DEALER STAFF —

SALES REP IN ALL CATEGORIES

★ Small value prizes in Scratch-and-Win cards for Sales Reps. The number of cards dispensed is proportional to the number of sales dollars generated. The higher the sales the more cards he/she receives.

★ Top Sales Rep in each of the three Dealer categories earns a trip to the Annual Convention and is recognized for their achievement with a gold plaque.

SERVICE TECHS IN ALL CATEGORIES

★ Small value prizes in Scratch-and-Win cards for Service Techs. The number of cards won will reflect the dollar value of service agreements sold plus dollar value of supplies sold. (If you have another measuring stick such as a testing program for technical knowledge of your products, then use it.)

★ Top Service Tech in each of the three Dealer categories earns a trip to Convention and is recognized for their achievement with a gold plaque.

ADMINISTRATIVE PEOPLE IN ALL CATEGORIES

★ Small value prizes in Scratch-and-Win cards for Administrators. The number of cards won can reflect a decrease in order processing corrections and the dollar value of supply sales generated. Many administrators take supply orders over the phone. The prizes should encourage them to make calls on their own and set up a telemarketing program in their spare time.

★ Top Administrator in each of the three Dealer categories earns a trip to Convention and is recognized for their achievement with a gold plaque.

ALL EMPLOYEES

★ Recognize years of service to the Dealership with service gifts reflecting the number of years of service. These years would be counted from the time the Dealership took on your product line.

Once again, it is important to recognize all high achievers at all levels of the Dealership. The employees contribute greatly to the success of your product line in the marketplace.

If you don't have an Annual Convention, consider starting one. Conventions are powerful inspirational vehicles. Recognize all the Dealers in one form or another. At a special dinner in their honour, acknowledge the highest achievers of Star Reach with speeches, plaques and a review of why they've won. Produce slides showing their smiling faces and their achievement. Let them each take a bow and be put in the limelight for a few minutes. Let them bask in their success.

The "Wall of Fame" at Head Office for the pictures of the Top Dealer Owners should be set up in a high traffic area. A second copy should be made up for the Dealer's office. A gold bar along the bottom of the picture would be engraved "(Dealership's name) inducted onto the Wall of Fame of xyz company, month, year)."

Another great idea is to take an imprint in cement of the shoes or hands of the "Wall of Fame" Dealers. These imprints could be made a part of your sidewalk or preserved for all time on the floor of your Wall of Fame Gallery. This wall or room will become a "must see" for all visitors.

Scratch-and-Win cards: It is most effective if the Sales Reps, Techs and Administrators receive their cards regularly - daily if you can or weekly if daily isn't possible. Whichever you choose, gather the troops together so that they can enjoy each other's successes. Regular dispensing of the cards provides immediate gratification, continued inspiration and builds team work.

You will have to entrust your Dealer Owners to keep the cards under lock and key. They are also accountable for the numbers given out. Each card should come with a dollar value. This way, the employees automatically earn something. By scratching away the stars on the cards, the employee can possibly double or triple the monetary value or win a prize. The prizes should be small, say under $10. Every 20th card could be printed with a high ticket item, ie; camera, disc player, briefcase, etc.

You could structure the program so that a rep will receive one card for every x thousand dollars in sales.

Administered properly, the cards will provide the interest needed to keep involvement and momentum going all year long. The catered-in office party allows everyone in the company to share in the dealership's successes and promotes comraderie, goodwill and positive attitudes.

THE PROGRAM LAUNCH

You may choose to launch Star Reach at your Annual Convention. Here are the tools that will provide the "WOW" you're looking for to make an immediate impression.

1) VIDEO: create a video that introduces Star Reach in a high excitement format. Outline how the Dealer structure works and what the program will provide to the Dealer Owner and his staff. The video can also be used to recruit new dealers.

2) FOLDER: The contents of the folder will recap the information from the video and provide all the details including prizes to be earned. Use the folder to recruit new dealers.

3) SALES CHARTS: These can be hung in the dealership's sales room. Use the same Sales Rep chart described in the program "Dream Trippers" (see index). The Dealership can mark the company's forecast goal for the year in terms of 3, 4 or 5 stars. He/she can also mark the sales goal for "Dream Trip" for the company. Each Sales Rep can use the same chart to plot his/her sales for the month to determine the number of Scratch-and-Win cards he/she will receive and the required sales attainment with respect to "Dream Trip" and the Annual Convention.

Use the same chart or create a separate chart to show the progress of the techs and administrators in terms of Scratch-and-Win and chances of making the free trip to Convention.

4) MIND JOGGERS: Every month or two have your program co-ordinator send out humorous reminders or mind joggers about the benefits of participating in Star Reach.

MEASUREMENT You'll begin to receive positive feedback from your Field Managers early in the first year. They will notice the interest level at current dealers and with dealers they're trying to recruit. However, it will take awhile to see the true benefit of Star Reach. After your second convention, you'll be able to see the effect of the program - the excitement, the comraderie, the loyalty and the sales. Your Dealers and their staff will want to sell your products versus competitive products simply because they're happier dealing with you.

After 6 months and then after one year, determine the participation level of the Dealers. Have your Dealer Field Managers call on the Dealers to recruit any remaining Dealers onto the program. The Dealers have nothing to lose - everything to gain. Determine the cost of the program as a % of total sales.

Following your first convention, analyze the progress of Star Reach. Are you meeting your objectives? Recommend changes, if any, to improve the program.

RECOGNITION

Earlier we discussed the power of recognizing the top achievers at an Annual Convention. Nothing can replace the pride generated by receiving recognition in front of your peers and staff.

There will be Dealers at convention who are not called up to the podium. They are those who are steadily building their business. Recognize everyone in the room in one way or another. After all, *they are all winners*. One way to do it is to have each Dealer's name and picture flashed for a moment onto an overhead screen using slides.

To inject some fun and feeling into the proceedings, give out awards for: The Best Poker Player, Mr. or Mrs. Sense of Humor, The Loudest Snore, The Most Beautiful Baby or The Sexiest Male Legs!

Another strong method of recognizing achievers is to publish their accomplishments in a journal of some description. One that I've used most effectively is a monthly newsletter. For details on how to design this newsletter, check out the program entitled "Star Reach - The Newsletter" (see index).

At the local level, the Scratch-and-Win cards for the reps, techs and administrators should be handed out at your daily or weekly sales meetings.

For all new Dealers entering into a different star category and for top Dealers in each category, have your company President/CEO and National Sales Manager send a letter of recognition and thanks to each and every employee at the Dealership. For added punch, send the letters to their homes so that the spouses can bask in the glory of their achievements.

NOTES

In this example, I've started the 3 star category at sales of $100,000. The categories for your company may change to be divided into fewer dollars or into millions of dollars. Whatever the split, consider having a "reach" for the new Dealer Owner in terms of sales required before he/she becomes a Star.

From year to year, add some spice by changing the prizes on the Scratch-and-Win cards or come up with another instant-win idea.

STAR REACH

Your name
Superstar
Sales Rep

Your name
Superstar
of Program
for Profits

Your name
Superstar
Sales Manager

Superstar
Technical
Service Rep

Your name
Superstar
Dealer Owner

Superstar
Branch
Administrator

Your name
Superstar
Branch Manager

BECOME A SUPERSTAR!

The names of the top individuals within each category above are featured on the page of this monthly newsletter.

Look inside for additional information on the 100% club achievers. Dream trippers, sales success stories, selling tips and more!

Company Logo

STAR REACH — THE NEWSLETTER

DESCRIPTION   No communication vehicle to your troops can top "Star Reach - The Newsletter". From cradle to grave, human beings love to see their name in lights. Star Reach - The Newsletter is a monthly publication which recognizes your top achievers, shares success stories and brings the strength of the organization into everyone's living room.

The details for this program show you how to set up the newsletter. There are suggestions for the types of awards that should be a part of your company's lifestyle.

An important side benefit is that this program is a tool for senior management with which to track the progress of the organization while keeping sales numbers confidential.

PARTICIPANTS   Field Sales Reps in Branch and Dealer offices, Dealer Owners, Branch Managers, Sales Managers, Technical Service Reps, Branch Administrators, all other company employees.

OTHER APPLICATIONS   Government employees, manufacturing.

OBJECTIVES   The newsletter accomplishes 3 things:
- ☑ it recognizes the top achievers within the various areas of your organization (see section "Awards Categories")
- ☑ it shares field success stories and sales tips with everyone in the country or your territory
- ☑ it shrinks the country. Once a month you share tidbits of info from employees/dealers across the country.

LENGTH   Ongoing monthly newsletter.

DETAILS   Appoint a Newsletter Coordinator who will be responsible for gathering and publishing the newsletter. The program may look very time consuming. Experience has taught me that with an organized info gathering system and a personal computer, the monthly newsletters can be produced quite quickly.

THE AWARDS CATEGORIES

Often, you will come across company newsletters that recognize the achievement of only the salespeople. I believe that the Service Technicians and Branch Administrators are equally as important to an organization as the sales people. It is these two individual groups who provide most of the after-sales service to your customer base. It is their responsibility to keep your customers happy. The Service Tech physically calls on the customers to fix/maintain their product. The Branch Administrator takes repeat supply orders, service calls, reduces receivables, keeps the branch inventory in check, accelerates the billing process and handles telemarketing for prospects.

The 90's decade is one in which we must improve productivity and vastly improve our customer service in order to keep the competition at bay. Treat your after-sales service employees with great respect.

Discussed below are 6 possible award categories:

SUPERSTAR SALES REP
The recipient of this award will be the Sales Rep in both branch and dealer operations with the highest dollar volume for the month. If you have different reps selling another different product line, you may wish to have 2 awards in this category. Do you have a National Accounts Sales force? If so, a third award is recommended for that category.

If your sales force consists of a group of young rookies and a group of very experienced reps, consider an award for each group. It's unfair to have the rookie compete against a 20 year veteran, unless you choose to seniority weight the sales results as per "U-TOP-IA" (see index).

Some companies will offer an additional award to reps for the sale of multiple units.

SUPERSTAR SALES MANAGER
Under this organizational structure, the Sales Manager's primary role is to train and motivate the troops to produce consistent sales results. There is a Branch Manager who oversees the Branch operations.

The recipient of this award can be the Sales Manager with the greatest dollar sales per rep. A second way to determine the winner is to choose the manager with the greatest percentage over his/her total territory forecast for the month or the greatest percentage over hardware forecast only.

SUPERSTAR BRANCH MANAGER AND SUPERSTAR DEALER OWNER
The recipients of this award will be the manager/owner with the greatest percentage over their total forecast for the month.

SUPERSTAR TECHNICAL SERVICE REP

I believe that the Service Reps should be recognized for the job that they were hired to do. Select the Superstar by measuring tangible things: number of calls in a day, number of call backs, mean time between failure rates, etc. You can also look at the number of service contracts sold or renewed and the dollar value of supplies and accessories sold if you can't measure the technical aspects.

SUPERSTAR BRANCH ADMINISTRATOR

The recipient of this award can be the Administrator with the best score in all or some of the following categories of responsibility: accuracy of inventory reporting, year-to-date admin. expenses (% of forecast), telemarketing sales (% of forecast) and receivables (day sales outstanding).

SUPERSTAR OF PROGRAM FOR PROFITS

This award will cover the rest of the people in the company. Every organization would love to cut costs and increase profits. All employees are encouraged to submit Programs for Profits, that is, any program that has the potential to increase company profits. If possible, they should show the potential dollar savings over the course of the year. A committee selects the winner in this category. The winner could be the one with the greatest $ savings or time savings.

WHAT DO THE AWARDS LOOK LIKE?

The biggest reward for each winner is to have his/her name up in lights for the world to see. I also recommend that you produce personalized plaques for each winner. Have the winner's immediate supervisor treat the winner to lunch.

This program need not be expensive - it's the name in lights that really turns people on. Oh, you can go whole hog if you like and hand out sweatshirts, pens, portfolios or whatever. But, they aren't necessary. One exception might be the Program for Profits award. If an employee is saving you big bucks, consider sharing the wealth.

WHAT DOES THE NEWSLETTER LOOK LIKE?

The ensuing pages graphically outline the make-up of your newsletter. You will notice that I've included pages for "The 100% Club", "Dream Trippers" and "Star Reach - a Dealer Program" (see index). Look at the programs that you're currently running and include them in the newsletter.

Have your local printer print up the template pages. The 1st. and second pages can be printed with blanks in the stars on the 1st page. You can fill those in every month. For the remaining pages, you can have the headings printed and the detail filled in every month. 2 colors for the front cover will add some zip.

You'll notice that I haven't included any $ figures on the pages. Just %'s. That way, you keep your total company sales confidential.

MEASUREMENT This Newsletter is an excellent program for tracking the progress of your organization.

Twice a year, ask you Managers to critique the Newsletter. Recommend changes, if any, since it is such a powerful vehicle, you will want to make sure it's doing the right job for you.

RECOGNITION The Sales Rep, Sales Manager, Tech Service and Branch Administrator awards must be presented by the Branch Manager or Dealer Owner at a local meeting. If the P for P Superstar is in Head office, then have his/her manager present the award at a lunch meet. The Dealer Owner and Branch Manager should receive their awards from their Managers - at their location, if possible.

All Superstars should receive a letter of recognition from the President/CEO and the individual in charge of their division. Or, take a copy of the Awards Page and have the Prez. hand write a note to each winner right on the Awards Page.

If you've implemented "Star Reach - a Dealer Program", you'll be recognizing your Dealers' achievements for the year at an Annual Convention. Publish a special page of the annual awards in the Newsletter as well.

NEWSLETTER FORMAT

Page 1 - Cover Page

STAR REACH

Your name
Superstar
Sales Rep

Your name
Superstar
of Program
for Profits

Superstar
Technical
Service Rep

Superstar
Branch
Administrator

Your name
Superstar
Dealer Owner

Your name
Superstar
Sales Manager

Your name
Superstar
Branch Manager

BECOME A SUPERSTAR!

The names of the top individuals within each category above are featured on the page of this monthly newsletter.

Look inside for additional information on the 100% club achievers. Dream trippers, sales success stories, selling tips and more!

Company Logo

Page 2 - Awards Descriptions Page

STAR REACH AWARDS

	Award Type	Branch Award	Dealer Award
☆ Superstar Branch Administrator	Plaque		✓
☆ Superstar Branch Manager	Plaque	✓	✓
☆ Superstar Dealer Owner	Plaque		✓
☆ Superstar Programs for Profit	Plaque	✓	✓
☆ Superstar Sales Manager	Plaque	✓	✓
☆ Superstar Sales Rep.	Plaque	✓	✓
☆ Superstar Technical Service Rep.	Plaque	✓	✓
☆ The 100% Club	Gold Pins, Pendants, Plaques, Diamond Rings, Certificates	✓	
☆ Dream Trippers	Exotic Trip	✓	✓
☆ Star Reach Dealer Awards	Plaques, Gifts, Media, Rebates, Co-op, VIP trips, Wall of Fame		✓

☆ IN THIS SPACE, GIVE A SHORT DESCRIPTION OF THE CRITERIA FOR ACHIEVING THIS AWARD.

Company Logo

Page 4 - Detail

SUPERSTARS

— ADMINISTRATION, P FOR P, TECHNICAL SERVICE —

ADMINISTRATION

Names   **Points or Totals**

List all names and the points they've achieved so that everyone can see the standings.

TECHNICAL SERVICE

Names   **Points or Totals**

List all names and the points they've achieved so that everyone can see the standings.

PROGRAMS FOR PROFIT

Give the Superstar's name and share his/her program with everyone.

Company Logo

Page 3 - Award Winners

SUPERSTARS — (Month, Year)

Superstar Branch Administrator - _____ (Name)

Superstar Branch Manager - _____ (Name)

Superstar Dealer Owner - _____ (Name)

Superstar Program for Profits - _____ (Name)

Superstar Sales Manager - _____ (Name)

Superstar Sales Rep - _____ (Name)

Superstar Technical Service Rep - _____ (Name)

100% Club Certificate Achievers - _____ (Name)

_____ (Name)

_____ (Name)

_____ (Name)

Company Logo

Page 5 - Detail

DREAM TRIPPERS

— REPS AND MANAGERS —

Sales Reps   Location   J F M A M J J A S O N D   YTD %

List the Sales Reps' names and locations. For each month, state the % sales achievement of the monthly trip quota and fill in the year-to-date percentage column. At all times, they will know their status.

Sales Managers   Location   J F M A M J J A S O N D   YTD %

(same process as Sales Reps above)

Company Logo

Page 6 - Detail

DREAM TRIPPERS

— DEALER OWNERS AND BRANCH MANAGERS —

Dealer Owners   Location   J F M A M J J A S O N D   YTD %

If you are using "Star Reach - a Dealer Program" (see index), divide this section into 3, 4 and 5 Star Dealers and track their progress within their star category. At the end of the year, print a special page showing all the awards from the Star Reach Dealer Program.

If you're not using the Dealer Program, simply follow the same process here as for the Sales Reps on Page 5 of this newsletter.

Branch Managers   Location   J F M A M J J A S O N D   YTD %

(see Sales Reps' Page - same process)

Company Logo

Page 8 - Success Stories

SHARING YOUR SUCCESS

On this page, have the Superstar Sales Rep and Sales Managers from the previous month submit a short story on why he/she was able to achieve Superstar of the Month. Did he/she make more calls? More demos? Re-organize his/her calling pattern, etc?

Selling Tips

Have the field submit selling tips that you can share with the troops.

Company Logo

Page 7 - 100% Club

100% CLUB

— SALES REPS —

Name **Location** **J F M A M J J A S O N D** **YTD Total**

List the Sales Reps' names and locations. For each month, state the number of points each month and their year-to-date total in the last column.

Certificate Winners (1st, 2nd, 3rd, 4th) Quarter

List the sales reps' names who received their certificates.

100% Club Achievers To Date

List the sales reps' names who have already achieved 100 points, 125 points and 150 points. Also mention what they are to receive (pin, pendant, plaque, ring, diamond, etc.).

Company Logo

PART D:

14 TESTED, DYNAMIC, SHORT-TERM INCENTIVE PROGRAMS

14 TESTED, DYNAMIC, SHORT-TERM INCENTIVE PROGRAMS

Short-term incentive programs can create the flurry of activity that you're looking for in a given time-frame. In fact, there are numerous benefits obtained from running short-term incentives. The attached chart lists 25 of them! Over half are people-related versus number-related. This reinforces the fact that incentives do more than just move numbers.

Once you've run a few of these incentives, you'll find that your people will look forward to seeing them year after year. Their competitive spirit will surface. The runner-up to any program will swear that they'll be #1 next year!

Use your creativity to add drama to these 14 short bursts of activity. People like hype. Some of the programs are 3-4 weeks in length while others run for 1 month, 2 months and 3 months. Each one will have your people and your Dealers and their staff eagerly awaiting the results.

**INCENTIVE PROGRAMS ARE
MASTERFUL BUILDERS OF PEOPLE.**

---

25 BENEFITS OF SHORT-TERM INCENTIVE PROGRAMS

People Benefits:
- Build teamwork
- Improve productivity and make this high productivity the norm once the program has been completed
- Improve quality of service
- Boost company morale
- Generate ideas for increasing productivity, reducing costs and increasing profits
- Expedite the learning curve of sales reps learning new products
- Obtain feedback from the front-line troops on the problems/opportunities in the field
- Get to better know your customer
- Improve rapport between the field and Head Office
- Instil competitive spirit within your organization
- Generate customer awareness of your company and its products/services
- Obtain free public relations by raising money for a national charity
- Overcome staff uncertainty during a merger or acquisition
- Recognize and praise the achievements of your staff
- TO HAVE FUN!

Number Benefits:
- Reduce costs
- Increase profits
- Focus on telephone sales
- Reduce receivables
- Accelerate the billing process
- Focus your Service Techs on selling service agreements and supplies when they're calling on current customers
- Increase the number of product demonstrations per day by your sales staff
- Focus attention on the sales of used equipment, obsolete inventory, or slow-moving products
- Increase sales during slow sales months
- Drive sales to meet year end's forecast

Chart #14

Spring Wings

ATLANTIC CITY — MONTREAL — RENO
LAS VEGAS — NEW YORK — NEW ORLEANS

Excel In Your Sales Performance and
Earn A Trip Location of Your Choice,
Cold Hard Cash and More!

Company Logo

SPRING WINGS

DESCRIPTION   Flush the Winter Blues away with this vibrant program. Board your top producers onto a set of wings and fly them away for a Spring holiday.

PARTICIPANTS   Field Sales Reps in Branch and Dealer Offices.

OTHER APPLICATIONS: The program's objectives and rules can be modified to suit:

1) Government Employees, Administrators, Plant Workers, Telemarketing Reps and Customer Support Employees: reward the best ideas for improving productivity, reducing costs and/or increasing profits. Increase your telephone sales, reduce receivables, accelerate billings, reduce manufacturing waste.

2) Service Technicians: reward an increase in the number of calls they make in a day, improve the quality of service, increase the sale of service contracts and lower-priced products (supplies, accessories, etc.).

3) All Employees: create or maintain a happy working environment. Generate ideas for increasing productivity, reducing costs and/or increasing profits.

4) Managers: improve productivity or sales per employee, create comraderie (a team) through friendly competition between managers.

This program can be run locally, regionally or nationally.

OBJECTIVES
1) To increase year-to-date sales (your sales are currently sitting below forecast).

2) To build comraderie and have some fun.

LENGTH   3 months

DETAILS   See the page entitled "Rules" for the program details.

The top producer for the three month period earns a spring holiday for two. The destination is his/her choice! Have each rep choose a location and record the locations on the sales boards in each office.

The second highest producer for the three month period earns a prize of their choice worth up to $800.

The Sales Representatives with the five highest extrapolated dollars *in each month* will receive a $100 gift certificate. Or, you may choose to give a gift certificate to the top achiever in each Branch/Dealership or Region. It really depends on the size of your organization.

MEASUREMENT   Determine what effect the program had on the Y-T-D sales and profit forecast. Compare sales and profits for this period, this year versus last.

Determine the participation level by dealer rep and branch rep.

Recommend changes, if any, to future programs. Determine the cost of the program as a % of sales generated.

RECOGNITION   Keep them pumped at your weekly sales meetings by recognizing the leaders and praising everyone's efforts.

Once a month, present the gift certificates to your top producers at one of your branch meetings. If there are no certificates earned at your location, take your top two people out for lunch.

If one of your people wins one of the top two prizes, have a party! Put your top producers in the limelight.

A recognition memo from the National Sales Manager and the President/CEO is a must.

SPRING WINGS

— RULES —

1. Spring Wings is open to all Sales Representatives in Branch Offices and within our authorized dealer network.

2. All Field Sales Reps' results will be seniority weighted as follows:
   Category A: Reps $\geq$ 2 years experience = $ Sale $\times 1.00\%$ = contest $ submitted
   Category B: Reps $\geq$ 1 year experience and < 2 years experience = $ Sale $\times$ 1.25% = contest $ submitted
   Category C: Reps < 1 year experience = $ Sales x 1.50% = contest $ submitted
   Weighting allows all reps the opportunity to win by giving the junior reps a bit of a head start over the more experienced reps who should find the selling game a lot easier.

3. FIRST PRIZE: The Sales Representative with the greatest extrapolated sales dollars for the contest period will earn $1200 towards a trip of his/her choice. The trip must be taken before (day, month, year).

4. SECOND PRIZE: The Sales Representative with the second highest extrapolated sales dollars for the contest period will earn $800 towards a prize of his/her choice.

5. BONUS PRIZES: The Sales Representatives with the five highest extrapolated sales in each month will each receive a $100 gift certificate to a fashionable mens or ladies clothing store.

6. Branch Managers/Dealer Owners are to submit to Head Office the names of their top five Sales Reps for each contest month, along with their real and extrapolated sales numbers. Submissions must reach Head Office by the third working day of the month following. See page entitled "Tally Sheet". Each month, Head Office will announce the national leaders in the race for 1st and 2nd prize and announce the winners of the gift certificates for the month.

7. The program runs for 3 months, beginning _____, _____.

Company Logo

SPRING WINGS

— TALLY SHEET —

	REAL SALES $	**EXTRAPOLATED SALES $**
FIRST PRIZE Name _____	_____	_____
SECOND PRIZE Name _____	_____	_____
THIRD PRIZE Name _____	_____	_____
FOURTH PRIZE Name _____	_____	_____
FIFTH PRIZE Name _____	_____	_____

Month of _____

Branch/Dealer _____

Manager's Signature _____

| Company Logo |

Next month you will be very warm in a new sweatshirt!

You will win your next racquetball game. Your prize: a new racquet!

Confucious say, you be very rich one day. You have just earned $100.

Tomorrow will be a happy day. Your prize: a gold watch!

You are luckier than an elephant's ear! Your prize: a calculator

Practise your chopsticks! You have earned a Chinese dinner for two!

Soon you will fall in love. Your prize: a romantic weekend for two!

Company Logo

KOOKIE KAPERS

DESCRIPTION   A "Kooky" of an idea! Fortune cookies and the mystique of hiding fabulous prizes inside the cookies will make this program an instant success. *"Kookie Kapers"* guarantees that your field force will quickly learn and sell new products.

PARTICIPANTS   Field Sales Reps in Branch and Dealer offices.

OTHER APPLICATIONS   The program's objectives and rules can be modified to suit:

1) Government Employees, Administrators, Plant Workers, Telemarketing Reps and Customer Support Employees: reward the best ideas for improving productivity, reducing costs and/or increasing profits. Increase your telephone sales, reduce receivables, accelerate billings, reduce manufacturing waste.

2) Service Technicians: reward an increase in the number of calls they make in a day, improve the quality of service, increase the sale of service contracts and lower-priced products (supplies, accessories, etc).

3) All Employees: create or maintain a happy working environment. Generate ideas for increasing productivity, reducing costs and/or increasing profits.

4) Managers: improve productivity or sales per employee, create comraderie (a team) through friendly competition between managers.

This program can be run locally, regionally or nationally.

OBJECTIVES: 1) Some Sales Reps go into shell shock at the launch of a new product. They're often intimidated by new products. Others are just too busy selling the old line. Use this program to inspire your troops to quickly learn new products. The faster they learn, the faster they'll sell new products.

2) Kookie Kapers provides the opportunity for field Sales Reps to become involved in a follow-up program to a national convention theme. If your national convention involves field management only, send the managers home with this program. To launch the program at the convention, each manager/dealer would receive a giant fortune cookie (with prizes inside) at their seating place on the convention floor.

Watch them get excited about taking the program home to their reps!

LENGTH   Three to four weeks

DETAILS   See attached ''Rules'' for most of the details.

Estimating the number of cookies you'll need to have made can be done using old call reports. Determine the average number of demos and sales made in a given week. If you don't have the call reports for dealer reps, make a few phone calls and estimate the number. There are lots of oriental fortune cookie manufacturers to be found. Have them make up *triple* the quantity you've estimated. You'll need a few fortunes to fill the pipeline; that is, you should send a stock of cookies in advance to each Branch Manager and participating dealership. As the program heats up, they can request that more fortunes be sent their way. Sending the fortunes in advance will allow the managers to be ready with the fortunes on the first day of the program.

Since this program is only three to four weeks long, keep boosting the reps' field activity by distributing the fortunes at the close of each day. It is very important that this contest be an instant-win as far as the cash is concerned. Watch them be energized for the next day!

As stated in the rules, the cash prizes are to be redeemed through the Branch Manager/Dealer Owner. Have them keep a stock of small bills on hand. They can then submit an expense form (attaching the ''fortune'' slip) to Head Office for reimbursement.

Branch Managers/Dealer Owners must submit a list of customers/prospects and products demonstrated/sold for the contest period. The number of fortunes distributed to the reps should equal the number of demos/sales completed as per Rules #1 and #2.

The cash prizes can be small ($5, $10, $20) with the odd fortune being seeded with $50 or $100 prizes. Merchandize prize ideas might be: gold pens, calculators, T-shirts, sweatshirts, sports racquets, watches, dinners for two at a local Chinese restaurant, etc. Your company's logo should be imprinted on the clothing.

MEASUREMENT Determine the increase in demonstrations/week compared to a week with no contest.

Determine the increase in number of demonstrations/sales for these products compared to previous new products launched.

Determine the cost of the program as a % of sales generated.

Did everyone enjoy the program?

Recommend changes, if any, to future programs.

RECOGNITION The reps will receive recognition in front of their peers at the close of each day, when the fortunes are distributed.

The beautiful part of this program is that everyone is truly a winner of cash or prizes. Each person is recognized for their hard work in learning new products.

Use the sales meeting as a time to discuss problems, opportunities and questions that the field may have with the new products.

Consider recognition for the individual who has earned the most fortunes per Branch/Dealer and/or for the entire country. A customized and personalized wooden plaque would be appropriate. A recognition memo from the National Sales Manager and the President/CEO to the top individual(s) is a must.

NOTES This program can also be used to move used equipment or current slow-moving inventory.

"KOOKIE KAPERS"

— RULES —

1. At the end of each program day, the Sales Reps will receive *one* fortune (cookie) for each *demonstration* of the new products A, B or C.

2. At the end of each program day, the Sales Reps will receive *three* fortunes (cookies) for each *sale* of the new products A, B or C.

3. Each fortune is seeded with valuable instant-win prizes for cash or prize slips for merchandise.

4. Redeem your merchandise slips by sending them in to the Marketing Coordinator at Head Office. Allow 2-4 weeks for delivery.

5. Cash prizes are to be redeemed through your Branch Manager/Dealer Owner.

6. The program runs for three weeks from _____, 19__ to _____, 19__.

7. All fortune prize receivers must be employees of the Branch or Dealership at the end of the program period.

8. Have fun and good luck!

Company Logo

U-TOP-IA!

DESCRIPTION   Lap top computers are a highly sought after item. Increase sales and have some fun with this simple but effective program. *"U-top"* all sales people and you'll win a lap top!

PARTICIPANTS   Field Sales Reps in Branch and Dealer Offices.

OTHER APPLICATIONS   The program's objectives and rules can be modified to suit:

1) Government Employees, Administrators, Plant Workers, Telemarketing Reps and Customer Support Employees: reward the best ideas for improving productivity, reducing costs and/or increasing profits. Increase your telephone sales, reduce receivables, accelerate billings, reduce manufacturing waste.

2) Service Technicians: reward an increase in the number of calls they make in a day, improve the quality of service, increase the sale of service contracts and lower-priced products (supplies, accessories, etc.).

3) All Employees: create or maintain a happy working environment. Generate ideas for increasing productivity, reducing costs and/or increasing profits.

4) Managers: improve productivity or sales per employee, create comraderie (a team) through friendly competition between managers.

This program can be run locally, regionally or nationally.

OBJECTIVES   To improve sales per rep for the slowest quarter of the year. In this case, summer is the slowest period. Other organizations might find January and February to be very slow.

LENGTH   3 months

DETAILS   See the attached "Rules" for the details of this program.

To your launch memo, attach a list of all the reps showing the category in which they will be competing.

Due to the length of the program, consider offering smaller prizes for the leader at the end of each month. Smaller prizes might be gold pens bearing the company logo, personalized portfolios, fashionable watches, etc.

Substitute prizes for the lap top could be a cellular phone or a video camera or a current rage high ticket item.

Field Managers may also be given the opportunity to participate. The manager with the greatest sales $ per rep for the contest period could win a top prize.

MEASUREMENT   Determine the increase in $ sales per rep over the same time period one year ago.

Determine the increase in total company sales over the same time period one year ago. How has this affected profits?

Determine the cost of the program as a percent of sales generated.

Did the field enjoy the program? Recommend changes, if any to future programs.

RECOGNITION   At the end of each month, praise all the employees as a group for their efforts. Special praise, of course, would go towards the leader who should receive his/her award amid applause from the other salespeople. He/she may take a few minutes to tell everyone how he/she achieved the sales for the month.

The *top achiever* at the end of the contest period should receive his/her lap top *computer* at a special sales meeting. Put the *U-top-ia* star in the limelight for awhile! He/she should be taken out for lunch.

All of these top achievers, monthly and quarterly, should also receive a congratulatory note from Head Office - National Sales Manager and the President/CEO.

U-TOP-IA!

— RULES —

1. The Sales Representative with the greatest contest $ submitted for the contest period will receive a lap top computer. He/she must be an employee with the company at the end of the contest period.

2. The sales results will be seniority weighted as follows:
   Category A: Reps $\geq$ 2 years experience = $ Sale x 1.00% = contest $ submitted
   Category B: Reps $\geq$ 1 year and $<$ 2 years experience = $ Sale x 1.25% = contest $ submitted
   Category C: Reps $<$ 1 year experience = $ Sale x 1.50% = contest $ submitted

3. The contest runs for 3 months from _____, _____ to _____, _____.

4. Sales of hardware, supplies and service agreements will apply.

5. Sales Representatives are to complete the contest form at the end of each month stipulating their real sales dollars and their contest $ submitted as per Rule #2 above.

6. Allow 4-6 weeks delivery for the lap top computer.

Company Logo

Hear Ye...
Hear Ye...

announcing the

Royal Marketing Academy

Triumph over all. Be one of this country's top achievers and you will descend upon the head office city for an unbelievably lavish 3 days of private limos, decadent dining, sightseeing and join the ranks of the prestigious few at the Royal Marketing Academy.

Company Logo

THE ROYAL MARKETING ACADEMY

DESCRIPTION
- Winners of this crème de la crème program will be treated like royalty with a trip to corporate Head Office. Winners feel special about being selected to visit the Executive Suites.
- Your top achievers become members of the Royal Marketing Academy - advisers to Senior Management. They will present their problems and opportunities to Senior Management with no filter screen/barrier, ie; middle management.
- Winners come from 3 areas of the company: Sales, Service and Administration.
- Of all the programs I've seen in my time, this one has to be the best motivator - the one that offers *recognition par excellence*.

PARTICIPANTS
Field Sales Reps in Dealers and Branch offices, Sales Managers, Service Technicians, Branch Administrators.

OTHER APPLICATIONS
This program can be modified to suit Government employees and all company employees. It can be run locally, regionally or nationally.

OBJECTIVES
1) This program provides Head Office with a very important vehicle to hear what is currently happening on the "street". Know your customer better by speaking directly to your field operations - the people who contact the customers on a daily basis. Field managers are usually in contact with headquarters on a regular basis. It's their front line troops you're after for this program. See the "Measurement" section for details on keeping the Field Managers in the loop.
2) To improve or maintain rapport between field staff and Head Office.
3) To increase sales, improve productivity, reduce inventories and receivables.

LENGTH
2 months

DETAILS
A considerable amount of planning is required for this superb program. Put your best detail person on the job.

WHO WILL ATTEND THE ROYAL MARKETING ACADEMY?

Since the main objective is to receive valuable input from the field, choose as many winners as are representative of your field force. I've seen this program run with 7-9 winners. 7 is the best number (it just so happens that 7 winners plus a couple of organizers fit well into a stretch limo!) One possible combination of Royal Winners could be:

(1) Top field Sales Rep. for product x
(2) Top field Sales Rep. for product y
(3) Top Dealer Sales Rep. for product x
(4) Top Dealer Sales Rep. for product y
(5) Top Sales Manager
(6) Top Service Technician
(7) Top Branch Administrator

It's important to include the Techs and Administrators in this program. They are *as valuable* to any company as the sales people.

HOW DO THEY WIN?

Choose measurements that are a stretch from the norm, yet attainable.

For example:

SALESPEOPLE Set a sales quota. The person with the highest $ over quota wins. To be fair, the individual results should be seniority weighted as follows:

Category A: Reps $\geq$ 2 years experience = $ sales x 1.00% = contest $ submitted

Category B: Reps $\geq$ 1 year and < 2 years experience = $ Sale x 1.25% = contest $ submitted

Category C: Reps < 1 year experience = $ Sale x 1.50% contest $ submitted

ADMINISTRATION This group can be measured on a combination of: age of inventory, inventory accuracy, order processing, corrections, number of charge backs, age of accounts receivable, etc.

SALES MANAGER The winner would have achieved the greatest $ per rep of the reps under his/her responsibility. Example: Sales Manager #1:

$100,000 in sales between 5 reps = $20,000/rep.
Sales Manager #2: $170,000 in sales between 7 reps = $24,286/rep. Sales Manager #2 will pack his/her bags.

SERVICE TECHNICIANS If you have a regular in-house testing program for service, then use it as your measuring stick. Ideally, the techs should be measured on the work they do (versus sales). Response times, call backs, number of calls in a day etc. are factors to consider. Another way to choose the winner might be dollar volume sales of service contracts and supplies.

THE HYPE

About one month before the contest period begins, send out little teasers to the field. One or two line memos are sufficient.

"Have you heard about The Royal Marketing Academy? Get the Royal Treatment for 3 luxurious days."

or

"Is blue blood running through your veins? Watch out for details of the Royal Marketing Academy."

At the same time, inform your field management of the program. They can hype it up.

To launch the program, you can either go wild (if you have a large budget) or you can tone it down. One company I know of had their marketing staff dress up as Royalty to pose for photographs in front of famous sights of the city. They used a collage of photographs to create a poster which was sent to the field. The winners could then get a feel for what they'd see when they arrived at the Head Office city.

Send the rules along with the poster. At two week intervals throughout the contest period, send updates or more pictures or "leak" some of the great things that they'll be doing in your fair city. Keep them pumped!

Once the winners have been selected, send a rose (yes, men like flowers too) with a congratulatory note. Advise the Branch Manager/Dealer prior to the flower's arrival so he/she can plan some local recognition. Send a memo to the field announcing the names of the winners.

THE AGENDA

Make their 3 day stay as exciting as possible! Hire someone to video tape the highlights because no one will believe them. Here's a suggested agenda befitting Royalty:

THURSDAY
11 a.m.

Winners arrive at the airport. Pick-up is in a limo with the company logo emblazoned on the door (magnetic signs work well if you've rented the limo). Magnetic flags bearing the company's logo can also be created to sit on the front fenders of the limo. Rent the limo for the 3 days. Champagne can be cooling in the limo's bar...

11:30 a.m.

Winners arrive at the best hotel in town. As they disembark from the limos, at the front of the Hotel are two trumpeters dressed in typical British garb and playing a fanfare. No, I'm not kidding! They will love the attention! A Town Crier, also in typical garb, is on hand to say "the Royal Marketing Academy welcomes (Town Crier shouts the names of the winners) to our fair city." The Town Crier can repeat this line for each winner as they disembark.

They, of course, are booked into the best rooms. Royalty never "checks in"! Have the Hotel Manager greet them at the entrance with their keys. Their luggage is delivered for them.

12:00 noon

Once the winners have freshened up, have them come down to an Executive Suite for the Welcoming Ceremony. A buffet lunch will be served at the Ceremony. Have the RMA (Royal Marketing Academy) wait in the foyer until all the winners have gathered. Inside the room is a gathering of company executives, the Mayor of the city and members of the Press. It's unlikely that your city will have had anything like this before — the Press will love it!

The Town Crier has been resurrected along with his Trumpeters. The Trumpeters play the fanfare once again. The Town Crier, with a large scroll in his hand, announces: "The Royal Marketing Academy of (your company's name) welcomes:
- the Cream of the Crop
- "A" Number One
- The Top of the Heap
- Apple of their Mother's Eye
- The Scourge of the Competition

- The Top Bananas
- La Crème de la crème
- And all around Great Folks

Ladies and Gentlemen please welcome ..." One by one, announce each winner's name by attaching "Lord" or "Lady" in front of each of their names, indicate the category in which they've won and their home town.

The President of the company now welcomes the R.M.A. He/she introduces the Mayor who presents each R.M.A. member with the keys to the city. Have huge 2 foot gold-painted keys cut out of foam core upon which is printed the city's name. The Manager who organized the program then provides the group with details of the next 3 days. Lunch is served!

2:30 - 6:30   Free time

6:30   Cocktails with Senior Management

7:00   Dinner. Have a sumptuous feast prepared befitting Royalty. This is a good time for the people to get to know each other. Some R.M.A. members could be shy about being placed face-to-face with the "Big Cheeses". Here's one ice breaker that'll be a roaring success. One company hired a "Royal Mime Artist". She is a superb comedian and had everyone in the room participating. Some R.M.A. members and Senior Managers became clowns for a time! Fun and laughter filled the room. As you can see, the mime artist broke the ice and set the tone for the remaining 2 days.
A "Royal Magician" or "Royal Juggler" could also work well.

FRIDAY
8 a.m.   Breakfast. An organizer or middle manager with whom the R.M.A. communicates on a regular business basis can be invited to join the R.M.A. for breakfast.

9 a.m.   Limo to Headquarters for a tour. Using either a portable sign or board sign, welcome the R.M.A. to Head Office. They'll be pleased to see their names in lights. The R.M.A. will enjoy visiting the complex, and meeting the people with whom they usually only chat over the phone. If you have a warehouse, make sure they see it. They are usually awed at the amount of inventory required to support the field.

NOON   Lunch at a restaurant that has English fare. If you have one that looks like a castle, take them there.

1:30-3:30   There are a variety of things you can do here:
- tour of the city (in a double decker bus?) by a hired guide
- theatre where Shakespeare is on the playbill
- tour of a famous local tourist spot, with or without a royal connection.
Whatever you do, add a personal touch to the event. Tea and scones with clotted cream and homemade strawberry jam is always a hit. Have one of the Head Office employees serve it to the R.M.A. in the limo prior to their departure for the afternoon event. Guaranteed to please!

3:30 - 6   Free time

6:00   Limo to the horse races.
British Royalty loves the horse races! You may not have the Ascot races in your city but your local race track will do. The better tracks have dining rooms where the R.M.A. and Senior Management can dine while watching the races. Provide betting money for a memorable evening.

Have a horse race named after your company. Take the R.M.A. down to the track for pictures with the winning horse.

SATURDAY
8 a.m.   Breakfast. A different middle manager can join them for breakfast.

9 a.m. - 3 p.m. The Royal Marketing Academy meets for the day. Having heard of and experienced different formats, I recommend one in which each R.M.A. has 30-45 minutes to make a presentation to Senior Management on the following:

1) What do they like best about working for this company?

2) What changes would make their jobs easier?

3) What products/services are their customers looking for?

The winners are to come prepared with visuals etc. Make sure you give them a couple of weeks notice prior to the R.M.A. in which to prepare. Make the environment friendly - a cosy room away from phones and interruptions.

Prior to this meeting, it is important to brief Senior Management on meeting conduct:
- listen carefully
- keep an open mind
- do not become defensive
- discussion should be soft, ask a lot of questions
- do not make on-the-spot decisions about issues.
It's vital that the R.M.A. feels their comments have been heard and are valuable to the company's future.

3 - 6 p.m.   Free time

6 p.m.   Arrange an exciting event where the entire company and their spouses/dates can join in the fun. How about a cruise boat complete with Mardi Gras band and buffet supper? Or, a medieval feast where everyone eats with their hands à la Henry the VIIIth? After supper, stage the Awards Ceremony. In front of their peers and the entire company, recognize each winner for his/her achievements:
- work history prior to and with this company
- 3 major accomplishments in life
- hobbies
- previous awards/trips won
- R.M.A. category and his achievement
- add funny stories about the winners that you have gleaned from managers, family, peers, friends, etc.

This information is to be obtained from the R.M.A. members prior to their arrival.

Special individual plaques with a Royal touch are a must.

SUNDAY a.m.   Breakfast and departure. Limo to airport. Since everyone will probably have different flight plans, you may wish to bring the trumpeters back for an official send-off at breakfast.

MEASUREMENT A few days after the Royal visit send a note to the winners asking for their feedback.

1) What did they like best about the Royal Marketing Academy?

2) What would they change to improve the program?

Take these suggestions seriously and consider implementing them into next year's program.

Record the problems/opportunities given at the R.M.A. and summarize the results for the Field Managers. It's important that the Field Managers/Dealer Owners do not perceive this as a program that overrides their responsibility and authority. They must buy into the program at the beginning and be informed of the results.

The R.M.A. will also be looking for implementation of some of their suggestions.

RECOGNITION You will have recognized the R.M.A. by:

1) sending them personal telegrams advising them that they have won

2) publishing a memo to the Field at large releasing the names of the new Royal Marketing Academy

3) acknowledging their achievements at the R.M.A. Awards Ceremony

4) sending each member a personalized letter from the National Sales Manager and President/C.E.O.

Throughout the year, consider recognizing them further by asking for their advice or assistance with product launches or business ideas. Some organizations will bring the R.M.A. in 3-4 times per year in order to obtain feedback on proposed new products and/or services.

(sample teaser)

THE ROYAL MARKETING ACADEMY

Will You Become a Member?

☑ Are you the best of the best?

☑ Do you have blue blood coursing through your veins?

☑ Are will willing to turn your briefcase in for a crown for 3 fabulous, fun-filled days?

☑ Will you be a member of the prestigious Royal Marketing Academy?

Company Logo

THE STEEPLECHASE!

ATTENTION: Sales Reps,
Service Technicians, Administrators,
Customer Service, Head Office Employees

SADDLE UP YOUR FAVOURITE HORSE
JOIN THE ENTIRE ORGANIZATION IN A
FUN-FILLED RACE TO THE FINISH!

Company Logo

THE STEEPLECHASE

DESCRIPTION   "Steeplechase" ranks high among the programs that builds teamwork. Run it during the last quarter of your fiscal year. Your sales will soar!

Can you imagine a race track set up to run the length of the hall of your corporate office? Can you imagine actual wooden horses "galloping" along your race track? This program is nothing short of inspirational. Everyone in the company gets involved to see the race to the finish. Try it, your employees will look forward to it year after year.

PARTICIPANTS   Sales, Service Technicians, Administration, and Customer Service support personnel, Head Office personnel - virtually everyone in the company.

**OTHER
APPLICATIONS**   This program's objectives and rules can be modified to suit Government employees and manufacturing as well. It can be run locally, regionally or nationally.

OBJECTIVES   1. To improve or maintain company spirit.
2. To build or maintain a team spirit.
3. To ensure that a sales forecast is met for year end.
4. To have fun.

LENGTH   3 months

DETAILS   See the attached "Rules" for details of the program.

Your Branches will be competing against each other. Of course, everyone in each Branch will want their team to win. The team work will be awesome.

Determine the # of Branches/Offices/Regions that will be participating. All offices should participate to ensure that no one feels left out. Dealers can also participate. If your Dealer network is huge, your race could become complex; however, it is still manageable. Every Dealer could have a horse, or, you can group the Dealers into Regions. Dealer Regions would compete against each other. Example: 8 dealers will represent the Western Region. The Dealer with the highest score in the winning Region or all Dealers in that Region achieving 100% or more of their contest quota will win a prize. Corporate Dealer Managers (who look after a Region of Dealers) can compete against each other.

To organize the race track:
- Have a local artist cut out little wooden horses (approximately 1 foot long by 8'' high). The horses must be able to stand up. They can be painted with jockeys on them. Each horse should have a # on it. Each Branch and Dealer Region will ''race'' a horse. Have one larger horse that represents the Corporate Sales target.
- Choose the location of your track carefully - the longer the stretch of floor the better. It could be located in a manufacturing plant, warehouse or the office. Using a removeable 1 1/2'' wide tape, mark your track as illustrated below, indicating the % of sales forecast achieved for the month.
100% 90% 80% 70% 60% 50% 40% 30% 20% 10% 0%
- The markings could be either on the floor or on the wall if your race track is near a wall.

Ensure that the quotas you establish are attainable but with a big enough stretch. Set up a tracking record to report race results weekly.

Pump up the adrenalin and anticipation by drawing names for the individuals at head office who will act as the ''jockeys''. Let each Region have a lot of fun in naming their horses. You'll get creative responses like ''BEST IN THE WEST'' and ''LEAN MACHINE''.

The prize money for Race No. 1 (your 1st. month) will be put up by each Branch or Region either from their ''kitty'' or individual contributions. I like the latter better. They will work harder when they realize that their own money is at stake (no pun intended!)

It is very important to ''run the race'' and move the horses each **week** . Mondays are good days. Choose one time every Monday so that everyone will look forward to that time. Ensure that the races are run weekly to build momentum and to keep the adrenalin flowing. Announce over the PA system when the next race will be run. Have as many employees as possible attend the race. Your ''jockeys'' will race the horses. Have one other employee race the corporate horse. Everyone will want to see where the company stands with respect to each month's target.

Always "Post" weekly race results immediately. Use your fax machine to inform everyone of the results. At the end of the month, send a memo recognizing the winners.

Encourage the jockeys to "ride" their Branches to bring in the sales. Every time they speak to the Branch they'll be encouraging them. Some will send ideas and various-in-sundry things to let the Branch know that they want to win!

Suggest that the winning prize money be used to organize a group event - dinners with spouses, rent-a-cruise for the evening etc. A group activity will reinforce the comraderie and team spirit.

MEASUREMENT Did everyone have fun?

Determine the participation level by group. Did all your employees and Dealers participate?

Determine the increase in sales of this quarter's results to last year's results for the same quarter. Did you make your sales year?

Determine the cost of the program as a % of sales.

Recommend changes, if any, to future programs.

RECOGNITION The frequent race results faxed to the field should keep everyone pumped.

Get the "trophies" out to the field as soon as you can. It's arrival will be another boost.

Encourage field management to hold inspirational meetings on a weekly basis. They can share ideas with their people on how they can help each other win.

Every employee in the winning Branch/Dealership should receive a letter of recognition from the National Sales Manager and the President/CEO.

At the end of the 3 races, have the President/CEO send out a general letter to all employees recognizing everyone's efforts in "The Steeplechase".

This program is a guaranteed winner.

NOTES: You may choose to run this program for only a certain group of employees. For example, Service Technicians can be measured on the sale of service agreements and supplies, sales leads, etc.

Since the program is such a powerful team motivator and builder, I recommend getting the whole company involved.

THE STEEPLECHASE
— RACE RULES —

1. The Steeplechase will run from _____, ____ to _____, ____.

2. Each of three races will be based on the attainment of total Branch/Dealer sales as compared to forecast. The Branch/Dealer with the highest % attainment wins.

3. To qualify for each race, the Branch/Dealer must be at least 100% of total sales forecast. The office with the highest percent over forecast will win the biggest prize for the month. Second and third prizes are available for those offices in the "Place" and "Show" categories.

4. Every Monday following the last week of business, Head Office Jockeys will run all Branch/Dealer horses along the Steeplechase track set up at Headquarters. Your horse will be placed at the spot representing your percent attainment of forecast.

5. In order to receive any prize money, individuals on the winning team must be employees of the company or its authorized Dealers at the close of each contest month.

Company Logo

THE STEEPLECHASE RACES AND PRIZES

RACE #1

	To Win	To Place	To Show
"THE INTRAC-TABLE PLATE"	65% of pot	25% of pot	10% of pot

Prize money is put up
by each Branch and
participating Dealer
($50)
Winning Branch/Dealer
will be awarded "The
In-trac-table Plate".
Winning "Jockey"
receives $75.

RACE #2

	To Win	To Place	To Show
"THE NATIONAL SALES MANAGER'S TROPHY"	$25 per Branch/ Dealer employee	$15 per Branch/ Dealer employee	$10 per Branch/ Dealer employee

Prize money is funded
by corporate Head
Office.
Winning Branch/Dealer
will be awarded "The
National Sales
Manager's Trophy".
Winning "Jockey"
receives $75.

RACE #3

	To Win	To Place	To Show
"THE PRESIDENT'S CUP"	$30 per Branch/ Dealer employee	$25 per Branch/ Dealer employee	$20 per Branch/ Dealer employee

Prize money will be
funded by corporate
Head Office.
Winning Branch/Dealer
will be awarded "The
President's Cup".
Winning "Jockey"
receives $75.

The "Triple Crown Trophy" will be awarded
to the Branch/Dealer winning all three races.

Company Logo

WHAT WILL PUT YOUR BRANCH OR DEALERSHIP IN THE WINNER'S CIRCLE?

SALES
- Make more cold calls
- Call your current customers - do they need a product upgrade or more supplies?
- Do more product demonstrations
- Organize local demothons (see index for "National Demothon Days")
- Hold product seminars for large groups
- Sell off used product
- Sell lots of new product
- Send out flyers

SERVICE
- Reduce your parts inventory
- Make more calls per day to reduce costs
- Sell supplies and accessories to the customers you service
- Sell service agreements

ADMINISTRATORS
- Reduce your inventories
- Reduce your receivables
- Sell supplies over the phone or use direct mail
- Help organize a "warehouse" sale to sell off used equipment

BRANCH MANAGERS/ DEALER OWNERS
- At weekly office meetings inspire your troops to win each race
- Organize a "warehouse" sale to move used equipment
- Call on major accounts. Encourage them to buy sooner
- Help the Sales Reps close tough deals

Company Logo

Santa's Christmas Bag

"Ho-ho-ho. Sell your socks off and I'll send you a complete new wardrobe from my bottomless bag."

Company Logo

SANTA'S CHRISTMAS BAG

DESCRIPTION Energize your troops at Christmas time! Your Field Sales Reps and Service Techs will eagerly participate in this program in which they can readily outfit themselves with a wardrobe from ''Santa's Bag''.

PARTICIPANTS Field Sales Reps and Service Tehnicians in Branch offices and Dealerships

OTHER APPLICATIONS: The program's objectives and rules can be modified to suit:

1) Government Employees, Administrators, Plant Workers, Telemarketing Reps and Customer Support Employees: reward the best ideas for improving productivity, reducing costs and/or increasing profits. Increase your telephone sales, reduce receivables, accelerate billings, reduce manufacturing waste.

2) All Employees: create or maintain a happy working environment. Generate ideas for increasing productivity, reducing costs and/or increasing profits.

3) Managers: improve productivity or sales per employee, create comraderie (a team) through friendly competition between managers.

This program can be run locally, regionally or nationally.

OBJECTIVES

1) Reduce stock of slow-moving hardware items through field Sales Reps.

2) Increase sales of accessories (add-on products), supplies and service agreements through field Service Technicians.

3) This short-term program is meant to facilitate top-of-mind product sales awareness for the Technicians whose primary job is to service equipment.

LENGTH 2 months. Run the program during October and November. They will then have their new ''duds'' in time for the holiday season.

DETAILS See the attached ''Rules'' for details of this program.

Contact a select few national clothing stores. If the contest is run nationally, you'll want gift certificates to stores that have locations across the country. This will lessen the coordination time necessary to acquire gift certificates. Arrange to have gift certificates created as soon as you can once the results are in.

MEASUREMENT Determine the increase in sales of these slow-moving products during this time period over the sales of the previous month.

Compare the increase in accessory, supply and service agreement sales.

Determine participation level by Dealer organization for both sales and service. Determine the # of direct Sales Reps and Service Techs who sold product under the program.

Determine the cost of program as a % of sales generated.

Recommend changes, if any, to future programs.

RECOGNITION Have the local Branch Manager/Dealer Owner present the certificates during an office meeting. Have the recipients talk about their successes. Praise everyone for their hard work.

Once the individuals have had time to purchase their wardrobe, have the Manager/Dealer Owner point out the new clothes that they're wearing and recognize them again for their hard work.

A recognition memo from the National Sales Manager and President/CEO is important.

SANTA'S CHRISTMAS BAG
— RULES —

YOUR RULES ARE EASY! Follow them carefully and you'll soon be wearing a new wardrobe from Santa's Christmas Bag!

1) SERVICE TECHNICIANS: Earn a $100 gift certificate for every $1,000 of sales in service contracts, supplies and accessories.

2) SALES REPRESENTATIVES: For every model A sold, receive a $25 gift certificate. For sales of models B and C, Santa will send you $20 and $15 certificates respectively.

3) Send in the attached "TAILOR-MADE" order form to: Santa: Head Office.
   BRANCH EMPLOYEES: Order forms must be accompanied by copies of orders.
   DEALER EMPLOYEES: Order forms must be accompanied by copies of invoices.

4) Order forms received by December _____, 19____ will find that Santa will deliver their new gift certificates in time for the Holiday Season.

5) Allow up to 6 weeks delivery for gift certificates if forms are not received prior to December ____.

6) Certificates are redeemable at the stores nearest you for (names of national clothing stores).

7) Contest runs for the months of October and November and closes November 30th.

8) All wardrobe recipients must be employees of either a branch or authorized dealership at the end of the contest period.

Company Logo

SANTA'S CHRISTMAS BAG

— Tailor Made Order Form —

Dear Santa:
During the months of October and November, I sold, leased or rented the following:

CUSTOMER NAME   PRODUCT $ VALUE

Grand total $_____

I have marked the dollar value of the certificates beside the name of the preferred store(s):

store x _____   store y _____   store z _____

Copies of order forms/invoices are attached.
Please rush me my gift certificates and Merry Christmas Santa!

Name _____
                     (please print)

Location _____

Manager's Signature _____

☐ Sales
☐ Service

| Company Logo |

N·A·T·I·O·N·A·L DEMOTHON DAYS

- Pre-arrange your product demonstrations for demothon day

- Do as many quality demonstrations as you can and win an evening of fine dining at your favourite restaurant

- Calls = Demos = Sales
  Be a top achiever!

Company Logo

NATIONAL DEMOTHON DAYS

DESCRIPTION   Your sales force in all parts of the country will create a flurry of activity in the marketplace. They will be conducting quality product demonstrations for a two day period. The team who does the most demos, wins an "Evening of Fine Dining" for four people.

PARTICIPANTS   Field Sales Reps in Branch and Dealer offices. Managers can also get involved. (see Rule #2).

OTHER APPLICATIONS: The program's objectives and rules can be modified to suit:

1) Government Employees, Administrators, Plant Workers, Telemarketing Reps and Customer Support Employees: reward the best ideas for improving productivity, reducing costs and/or increasing profits. Increase your telephone sales, reduce receivables, accelerate billings, reduce manufacturing waste.

2) Service Technicians: reward an increase in the number of calls they make in a day, improve the quality of service, increase the sale of service contracts and lower-priced products (supplies, accessories, etc.).

3) All Employees: create or maintain a happy working environment. Generate ideas for increasing productivity, reducing costs and/or increasing profits.

4) Managers: improve productivity or sales per employee, create comraderie (a team) through friendly competition between managers.

This program can be run locally, regionally or nationally.

OBJECTIVES

1) To encourage the field reps to conduct professional demonstrations of their products.

2) To accelerate the learning process by the Sales Reps for newly launched products.

3) To target a certain industry, ie; medical, manufacturing, etc.

4) To improve upon the number of demonstrations conducted per day per rep.

5) To create sales resulting from their demonstrations.

6) To encourage participation by Dealer Reps - it's often difficult to pique their interest if they sell several brands of the same product.

7) To build a mailing list of prospective customers.

8) To build teamwork among senior and junior reps.

LENGTH   Two days.

DETAILS   See the page entitled "Rules" for details.

Give your field managers at least three weeks notice of the Demothon Day. The reps will need this time to pre-book demonstrations.

If you think that your sales force will simply run like mad for two days and not do quality demonstrations that will lead to sales, then consider an optional type of contest. As per "OPTIONAL RULE #4", the reps can still compete in teams. The difference between the contests is that in the "Optional" one, the contest is no longer dependant on the number of demos. A secret time is chosen and the team having conducted the demonstration closest to the secret time, will be the winning team.

Another option to consider is that the prospect to whom the winning team gave the demonstration also wins a prize. The company will certainly remember you the next time they're in the market for a product. In some cases, however, companies and government organizations do not allow their employees to accept prizes.

MEASUREMENT   Measure the results of the program against your objectives ie number of demos per rep, number of hot prospects, number of sales, cost of the program per demo.

Determine the participation level by Branch and by Dealer.

Did they enjoy themselves? Recommend changes, if any, to future programs.

RECOGNITION   Branch Managers/Dealer Owners should recognize the efforts of all the Sales Reps at a sales meeting.

The team winners should receive their gift certificates in front of their peers amidst applause.

Send recognition letters from Head Office - one from the National Sales Manager and one from the President/CEO.

NATIONAL DEMOTHON DAYS

— RULES —

1) The contest days are _____ and _____, 19____ and is open to Sales Representatives in all Branches and authorized Dealerships.

2) All Sales Representatives are to be paired up in teams. Managers can participate to even up the teams.

3) Each team will consist of a team leader and another rep. The leader will be the rep whose territory in which the calls are being made. The partner will be a junior rep. On the second day of the contest, the team will move over to work in the junior rep's territory.

4) The teams, one in the East, one in the West, with the most product demonstrations in one day will each win an "Evening of Fine Dining" for four (retail value $200).

5) Fax the team results to the Marketing Coordinator at Head Office no later than noon of the day following each contest day.

OPTIONAL
RULE #4

A secret time has been chosen by the Company's Accountant, ____(name)____. Each of the two teams, one in the East and one in West, having conducted the demonstrations closest to the secret time will win an "Evening of Fine Dining" for four (retail value $200).

Company Logo

NATIONAL DEMOTHON DAYS

— CONTEST FORM —
(PLEASE PRINT)

Product Demonstration to

Customer Name _____

Customer Address _____

Customer Phone # _____

Customer Fax # _____

Time of Demonstration _____

Customer's Signature _____

Rep's Name _____ Reps' Signature _____

Branch/Dealership_____

Product Demonstration to

Customer Name _____

Customer Address _____

Customer Phone # _____

Customer Fax # _____

Time of Demonstration _____

Customer's Signature _____

Rep's Name _____ Rep's Signature _____

Branch/Dealership_____

Product Demonstration to

Customer Name _____

Customer Address _____

Customer Phone # _____

Customer Fax # _____

Time of Demonstration _____

Customer's Signature _____

Rep's Name _____ Rep's Signature _____

Branch/Dealership_____

Manager's Signature_____

| Company Logo |

AUCTION BUCKS

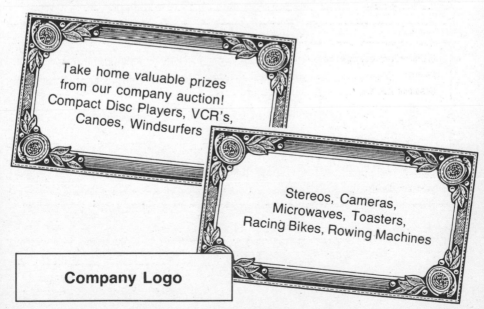

Take home valuable prizes from our company auction! Compact Disc Players, VCR's, Canoes, Windsurfers

Stereos, Cameras, Microwaves, Toasters, Racing Bikes, Rowing Machines

Company Logo

AUCTION BUCKS

DESCRIPTION Everybody loves a bargain! People who attend auctions speak with as much animation as the fisherman whose 3 footer got away! During the course of this program, the participants earn funny money (Auction Bucks). At the end, there is a huge auction organized just for them. They can bid on anything they like by using their Auction Bucks. It's fun, it's hilarious and it works. Try it!

PARTICIPANTS Field Sales Reps in Branch and Dealer offices.

OTHER APPLICATIONS: The program's objectives and rules can be modified to suit:

1) Government Employees, Administrators, Plant Workers, Telemarketing Reps and Customer Support Employees: reward the best ideas for improving productivity, reducing costs and/or increasing profits. Increase your telephone sales, reduce receivables, accelerate billings, reduce manufacturing waste.

2) Service Technicians: reward an increase in the number of calls they make in a day, improve the quality of service, increase the sale of service contracts and lower-priced products (supplies, accessories, etc.).

3) All Employees: create or maintain a happy working environment. Generate ideas for increasing productivity, reducing costs and/or increasing profits.

4) Managers: improve productivity or sales per employee, create comraderie (a team) through friendly competition between managers.

This program can be run locally, regionally or nationally.

OBJECTIVES
1) To increase sales during a traditionally slow month.
2) To direct sales towards slow-moving products and/or used products.
3) To build comraderie and have some fun.

LENGTH 1 month. This is a great program to hold every year during your slowest month. The reps will get quite fired up over it.

DETAILS   Each Branch or Dealership should run their own program.

Design a camera-ready sheet of Auction Bucks. The Field Manager can photocopy the sheets, cut them up and hand out the "bills" once they're earned.

Each location should set a goal of the sales they'd like to generate for the month. That goal should be much higher than the forecasted revenue.

You'll need to look at your product line and determine how many Auction Bucks should be awarded for the sale of each product. The higher the dollar value of the sale, the more Auction Bucks should be awarded.

Choose small but valuable prizes. Buy them and display them right at the beginning of the program. Some ideas for prizes are: gift baskets (food, wine, automotive, garden, etc.), briefcases, toasters, rowing machines, racing bikes, microwaves, watches, cameras, sports equipment, compact disc players, video cameras, portable phones, etc.

To be as fair as possible, you may wish to use the seniority weighting described in Rule #2 of "U-TOP-IA" (see index).

Keep a tally on your sales board of the Auction Bucks that have been won. At your weekly sales meeting, hand out the Bucks.

Hold your Auction at the close of business for the month once you've handed out the remaining Bucks. The reps will use their Bucks to bid on the prizes. You may choose to hold the Auction off-site where you can have a pizza and beer party after the Auction. Invite spouses/guests. Your sales people will then have their peers and loved ones around them with whom to celebrate their success.

MEASUREMENT   Determine what % of your sales goal you've achieved.

Determine the participation level by Branch and by Dealer. If they liked it, why? If they didn't, why not?

Determine the cost of the program as a % of sales.

Recommend changes, if any, to future programs.

RECOGNITION   The reps will be recognized weekly when they receive their Auction Bucks at your sales meetings. They will also receive recognition daily as they mark their sales on the Sales Board.

At the Auction itself, everyone will be a winner as they use their Auction Bucks to bid on the prizes.

NOTES   If your product line is a long-sell, you could dispense x number of Auction Bucks for product demonstrations. Experience teaches that the more demos you do, the more sales you make.

UNDER ~~COVER~~ COVER AGENT

Uncover the news of the name of our
new company . . . Tell the world
about our recent acquisition and
you could win valuable prizes!

Company Logo

UNDERCOVER AGENT

DESCRIPTION
I have never seen a better program for boosting company morale and building team work. I believe the reason is due to the fact that everyone in the company participates. In addition, Undercover Agent is outstanding as an inexpensive awareness builder for your company.

This program is ideal for an organization that is:
1) Going through a name change.

2) In the process of a merger or acquisition.

3) A brand new company.

4) In need of a morale boost.

PARTICIPANTS
Everyone on the company's payroll including the Big Cheese (President/CEO). Your Dealer organization will also love this program.

OBJECTIVES
1) Whenever major changes take place in an organization, employees are unsettled. They may feel insecure about their jobs, about the reporting structures and about the overall well-being of the organization. This program goes a long way towards making the employees feel a part of the "new" company. They will feel less threatened and their company pride will show through.

2) This program is a catalyst for building or maintaining team-work.

3) Undercover Agent is a masterful inexpensive advertising vehicle for your new company.

4) This program will raise money for your co's favourite charity. Your image in the marketplace will improve - you are now putting something back into the community.

5) You can use this program to build a powerful prospect list, if your conscience will allow it.

LENGTH
1 month.

DETAILS
The idea behind U.A. is to have every employee introduce your (new) company to as many people ("contacts") as they possibly can in a one month period - on or off the job. The "agents"

will carry with them a stock of pamphlets. The pamphlet is divided up into 5 sections:

1) The history of your (new?) company and a description of its products and services.

2) A few words on the program and its goals.

3) A coupon (see details below) to your fast food outlet.

4) A section dedicated to your charity. Describe the charity and your commitment to raise money for them. Your company will donate money (say $.50) for every signature received. The people contacted can also make a donation if they so desire.

5) An area where the "agent" can have his/her contacts place their signature. Before the signing, ensure that the "agents" inform the contact of the history of your company, what your products/services are, the charitable link and the value of the coupon.

When designing the pamphlet, sections 3, 4, and 5 above must be perforated. The "agents" will remove section 5 with the signature and leave the pamplet with the contact.

The details for planning Undercover Agent can be divided up into 3 major areas: Affiliated Organizations, Contest Design and Prizes and Support Materials.

AFFILIATED ORGANIZATIONS

If your company is new or has gone through a name change or merger/acquisition, you probably are faced with an identity crisis. People simply have trouble identifying your company with a product or service.

If your company has a charity that they support, use Undercover Agent to raise money for that cause. If you don't have a charity, find one. Children's foundations are usually good ones since every one of us either has children or has children in our circle of friends. Affiliating your company with a charity shows that you care about the community you live in - you are putting something back into it. For every signature received, your company will make a donation (say $.50/signature) to the charity.

Next, find a major fast food outlet that will trade your free advertising for a discounted food coupon. Associating your company's name with a large, reputable food chain will pyschologically put you into the big league with the contacts you make under this program.

CONTEST DESIGN AND PRIZES

First, determine how many signatures you think is attainable. Use 100 signatures per employee as a guideline. Some employees will gather very few whereas others will go crazy. I know of one situation where three employees gathered over 1,200 signatures each, two of which hit over 1,500!

Next, you need team leaders. A suggested list of "Bureau Chiefs" might be:

CATEGORY	BUREAU CHIEF
1. Dealer Operations	National Sales Manager for Dealer Operations
2. Branch Offices	National Sales Manager for Branch Operations
3. Head Office	Choose 4 Senior Managers from Finance, Admin., Service and Manufacturing

Give the Bureau Chiefs funny nicknames like "Peter Pan", "009", or "the Four Musketeers" for the Head Office Chiefs. These three categories are going to compete against each other to see whose team can collect the most signatures. If you only have Branch offices, then divide them up into teams with Bureau Chiefs assigned to each team.

To add to the fun, design giant "Peoplemeters" upon which you will mark the progress of each team. The Peoplemeters are simply 7 foot thermometers with graduations of team's goals printed up the side. Hilarious caricatures of each team leader can be sketched onto the Peoplemeters. The meters should be placed in a high traffic area of the company. Every Monday morning, gather the troops to watch the marking of the People meters and chart the progress of each team. You will not believe the competitive instincts of your people!

To set the targets for the Bureau Chiefs, count the number of employees in each of their areas. That number divided by the total number of company employees will be the % of the target signatures for each Category:

	(A) # of employees	(A) as a % of 1200 employees
Category #1	200	17%
Category #2	600	50%
Category #3	400	33%

Total # of employees = 1200

Therefore, Category #1 will carry 17% of the target # of signatures.

In Category #3, the 4 Bureau Chiefs will be competing against each other and as a group against Categories #1 and #2. If Category #3 wins, the Bureau Chief with the greatest # of signatures will win the largest bulk of the prize (say 60%). The other three chiefs can split the remaining 40%.

Next, organize all the employees so that they are also competing against each other in categories to win valuable prizes. Visual #4 lists suggested prize categories and prizes. Fill in the blanks on the last two columns to inform the agents of how many prizes can be won. For Field Managers and Dealer Owners, it is fair to have them compete on the number of signatures received per agent in their territory/office. Example: If Manager X has 55 agents in his territory working for him and his team brings in a total of 3,000 signatures, then he has achieved 54.5 signatures/agent. Other Managers will have to beat that number to win the prize.

THE SUPPORT MATERIALS

Your program launch materials will consist of:
1) Pamphlets.
2) Visuals (see attachments)
3) Optional cassette tape. Your can create a humourous tape of instructions for the program. You know the kind I mean...it ends with "This tape will self-destruct in 10 seconds"! You Field Managers/Dealer Owners must launch the program with great excitement. Think about sending the materials in a locked box which they will place in a prominent spot in each office. Only on the specific planned launch day will you give them the combination to the lock. They will be beside themselves with curiosity! One company that ran this program had so much success that they had to reprint the pamphlets 3 times. Make sure that you print twice

as many as the projected number of signatures. You'll need them to fill the pipeline.

MEASUREMENT   Determine the success of the program in terms of:
- did it boost the company morale?
- did you see improved team work?
- did you receive recognition for your charitable donations?
You will definitely have built awareness for your company.

Analyze the cost of the program versus your budget.

Determine participation level by employee and by dealership.

Recommend changes, if any, for the next time.

RECOGNITION   The recognition ceremony for each of the winners should be a special event. Where possible, Head Office Senior Managers should travel to the Field to present the prizes. If that's not possible, the local Manager should do the honor and a VIP memo from the President/CEO and the National Sales Manager should follow.

The President/CEO should send a general memo to everyone in the company thanking them for their participation and recognizing them for their efforts. The employees should know how much money they raised for the charity.

(SEE 1 - 6 VISUALS)

UNDERCOVER AGENT
— THE GOAL —

During the past few months, our company has undergone a major change. Three companies have merged to form one new company.

To celebrate this integration, our new company is getting everyone involved. Our mission is to have all employees, from coast to coast, talk about our new identity. From sales to service, branches and dealers, administration, manufacturing, head office support — everybody is a part of our mission.

We're determined to uncover over _____ contacts, tell them who we are and where we're going. This is our goal.

_____ SIGNATURES!

VISUAL #1

Company Logo

UNDERCOVER AGENT
— THE TEAM —

DEALER OPERATIONS	BRANCH OFFICES	HEAD OFFICE
(Name) - Bureau Chief - (Nick Name)	(Name) - Bureau Chief - (Nick Name)	(Name) - Bureau Chiefs - (Nick Name)
Special agents are all dealer employees: - dealer, Sales Reps. - dealer Sales Mgrs. - dealer Owners - dealer Administrators - dealer Service Reps. etc.	Special agents are all branch employees: - company Sales Reps. - company Sales Mgrs. - Branch Mgrs. - company Administrators - company Service Reps. etc.	Special agents are all head office employees divided into 4 categories: Finance Administration Sales and Marketing Manufacturing

Visual #2

Company Logo

SPECIAL AGENT PRIZES
DOZENS OF VALUABLE PRIZES TO BE WON

- TOP AGENT(S) IN EACH CATEGORY — Large Screen Color TV
- RUNNER-UP AGENT(S) IN EACH CATEGORY — Disc Player
- TOP BUREAU CHIEF — Cash! $2,000!

Visual #3

Company Logo

UNDERCOVER AGENT
— PRIZES BY CATEGORY —

Category	Cash	# of Large Screen TV's To Be Won!	# of Disc Players To Be Won!
1. Branch Managers			
2. Dealer Owners			
3. Branch Administrators and Service Coordinators		_____	_____
4. Service Technicians		_____	_____
5. Sales Managers		_____	_____
6. Sales Reps.		_____	_____
7. Head Office		_____	_____
8. Bureau Chiefs	$2,000	_____	_____

Visual #4

Company Logo

SECRET AGENT INSTRUCTIONS

- Tell everyone you know/meet about our new company and its new products.
- Have them sign the pamphlet to indicate that they now know about our story and our goal.
- Tell your contact that your company is raising money for (name and describe the charity). For every signature we receive during the undercover operation, our company will donate 50¢ towards the charity.
- Advise the contacts that they too can also make a monetary contribution to the charity by filling in the form on the pamphlet.
- Fax in the signature cards from the pamphlets.
- Very soon you may be enjoying your large screen T.V. or disc player!

Note: Any sales leads can be passed on to the appropriate Branch or Dealer.

Visual #5

Company Logo

UNDERCOVER AGENT — Who Do You Contact?

• Family/Friends • Your Spouse's Co-Workers • Customers • Prospects • Sports Teams: Hockey, Baseball, Weight Lifting, Rowing, etc. • Members of Associations You Belong To • Your Hair Dresser/Bank Teller/Doctor/Lawyer/Accountant • Chambers of Commerce • Sales Clubs • All Adults Over 18 Years of Age • Etc!

BE CREATIVE! — TELL THE WORLD ABOUT UNDERCOVER AGENT

Visual #6

Company Logo

Ten "Celebrities" will walk the famous fairways and join pro golf's Who's Who list for 4 glorious days.

Company Logo

THE PRO GOLF CELEBRITY CLASSIC

DESCRIPTION   Did you know that 60% of today's managers either play golf or are interested in the sport? Did you know that 40% of all new players are women? For these reasons, the offer of a trip to any prestigious golf tournament on the professional golf circuit will leave your Dealers and Managers salivating in anticipation. The Celebrity Classic with its presence of golf's Who's Who, the high-spirited evening festivities, the red carpet accommodations, golf privileges on world-class courses and the congenial comraderie of fellow "Pros" will carve lifelong impressions in the minds of the winners.

PARTICIPANTS   Dealer Owners, Branch Managers, Senior Company Managers.

OTHER APPLICATIONS   VIP customers from your major accounts.

OBJECTIVES
1) To reward your highest achievers (the "Celebrities") with a special event.
2) To instil a competitive spirit that will drive sales and profits.
3) To focus attention on certain products and/or services.

LENGTH   3 months.

DETAILS

RULES
Each participant needs a goal and the goals may be different depending on the size of their business or the potential. Whatever the goals are, make sure that they're fair to everyone. The goals can be units sold or dollars sold.

Ten winners, or more, if you can swing it (pun intended!), with the highest % over their goals, will join the ranks of the privileged few and attend an exciting all-expense paid excursion to your golf location.

THE PRIZE
Make the trip one of the highlights of their year. Here is a suggested agenda:

DAY 1

Noon - 6 p.m.   Arrival at airport. Chauffeur-driven limousine to an exclusive hotel at or near the tournament site. Fruit baskets and champagne in the rooms. Welcome Packages in their rooms with golf balls, visors, tees, towels, lapel pins with Celebrity Classic logo.

6:30 p.m.   Cocktails.

7:00 p.m.   Dinner with President/CEO of company.

DAY 2

8 - 9 a.m.   Breakfast.

9 - 5 p.m.   Walk the fairways and enjoy the 1st. day of the Tournament.

6:30 p.m.   Cocktails.

7:00 p.m.   Dinner with a Pro Golfer. Perhaps a 1/2 hour speech by the Pro.

DAY 3

8 - 9 a.m.   Breakfast.

9 - noon   ''Celebrities'' play golf.

1 - 4 p.m.   Walk the fairways and enjoy the 3rd day of the tournament.

5 - 6 p.m.   Golf clinic given by a Pro Golfer.

7 p.m.   Cocktails.

7:30 p.m.
- Theme specialty dinner.
- Entertainment (singers, dancers, magicians, jugglers etc.).
- Prizes awarded to Celebrities with the best score for the morning's golf game.

DAY 4

8 - 9 a.m.   Breakfast.

9 - noon   ''Celebrities'' play golf.

1 - 4 p.m.	Walk the fairways and enjoy the final round of the Tournament.

7 p.m.   Cocktails.

7:30 p.m.   Awards Banquet

Following a sumptuous sit-down dinner, the awards banquet begins. Each ''Celebrity'' is recognized for his/her sales/profits achievements and receives a momento of the event. Choose elegant prizes: pedestal or mantel clocks, sculptures, crystal, etc. The Awards Ceremony could include slides with pictures and the history of each of the ''Celebrities''.

Hire a photographer to take pictures of each presentation.

DAY 5

After breakfast, depart for home having experienced the magic of a Pros' swing.

MEASUREMENT Determine the impact of the program on sales, this quarter versus last and year-to-date versus last year, year-to-date.

Determine participation level by Dealer/Manager. From those who didn't participate whole-heartedly, find out why.

Determine the cost of the program as a % of sales.

Recommend changes, if any, to future programs.

RECOGNITION Throughout the contest, every 2 weeks if you can, send a contest memo to the participants showing their ''score'' to date.

At contest's end, a phone call from Head Office to the winner will pump up the adrenalin for the rest of the day. Follow-up the phone call with a recognition memo from the National Sales Manager and the President/CEO.

Send an eye-catching memo to everyone in your organization congratulating the winners and publishing the contest results.

The biggest recognition is the prize itself and the Awards Ceremony.

The Legendary Lotto

Become a legend. Prove that the summer months are the best months to sell. For every product demonstration and sale, you will earn valuable tickets which will be thrown into the Legendary Lotto hat. If your ticket is pulled, you will win your choice of a host of valuable prizes!
It's easy! It's fun.
It's Legendary
Lotto.

Company Logo

LEGENDARY LOTTO

DESCRIPTION   A personalized fun way to keep your employees hopping during the hottest time of the year ''weather-wise'' and usually
the coldest sales-wise! Participants receive ''tickets to win''
valuable merchandise - their choice!

PARTICIPANTS   1) Field Sales Reps in Branch and Dealer Offices.
2) Field Sales Management.

OTHER   The program's objectives and rules can be modified to suit:
APPLICATIONS: 1) Government Employees, Administrators, Plant Workers,
Telemarketing Reps and Customer Support Employees: re-
ward the best ideas for improving productivity, reducing
costs and/or increasing profits. Increase your telephone
sales, reduce receivables, accelerate billings, reduce
manufacturing waste.

2) Service Technicians: reward an increase in the number of
calls they make in a day, improve the quality of service,
increase the sale of service contracts and lower-priced
products (supplies, accessories, etc.).

3) All Employees: create or maintain a happy working environment. Generate ideas for increasing productivity, reducing
costs and/or increasing profits.

4) Managers: improve productivity or sales per employee, create comraderie (a team) through friendly competition between managers.

This program can be run locally, regionally or nationally.

OBJECTIVES   To boost sales during a traditionally slow period. If your sales
are high during the summer, use this program to encourage
emphasis on new products, over-inventoried product or used
equipment.

LENGTH   2 months, July and August.

DETAILS   See the attached ''Rules'' for details of this program.

Have some fun by personalizing the program. Name it after
someone in your company. For example, you could include
the National Sales Manager's caricature on the artwork for the
program.

As support material, all you need is a one-color poster announcing the program. The poster should be hung in each sales room across the country. Design the poster to include pictures of the merchandise. The reps and Sales Managers will look at the poster every day to see what they can win. It's important that they dream a little - they'll work harder. Typeset the "Rules" right on to the poster. All you'll need to add is a motivating cover letter.

The Branch Manager's Weekend-for-Two could include 2 nights of luxury accommodation, 3 meals daily, an evening at a concert or theatre, a sporting event and breakfast in bed! Retail value = $500.

The merchandise prizes can vary in value from $30 to $150. Some ideas are: mantel clocks, diamond pendants, cameras, pool tables, china, crystal, silver coffee carafe, stereo, rings, etc.

MEASUREMENT   Determine the effect of the program on sales and profits for this two month period over the same period last year.

Examine the participation level by dealer and branch rep.

Examine the most popular prizes and unpopular prizes.

Determine the cost of the program as a percent of sales.

Recommend changes, if any, to future programs.

RECOGNITION   After each weekly draw, send a memo to the field at large, recognizing the winning Sales Rep. Do it by fax or electronic mail - it's faster.

The Branch Manager/Dealer Owner should recognize the efforts of all his/her Sales Reps in a meeting format.

Every two weeks send an update to the Sales Managers and Branch Managers indicating their status. Each weekly winner as well as the top Sales Managers and top Branch Managers should receive a letter of recognition from the National Sales Manager and the President/CEO.

FAX TO: THE MARKETING COORDINATOR OF

THE LEGENDARY LOTTO

☑   Yes, Enter my Tickets-to-Win into THE LEGENDARY LOTTO HAT!

THE LEGENDARY LOTTO TICKET-TO-WIN

☑ Yes, enter my ticket-to-win!

Sales Rep's Name ☐ DEMO

_____ ☐ SALE

Co. Name of Sale/Demo _____

Address _____

_____

Model # _____

Date of Sale/Demo _____

Branch Mgr./Dealer Owner Signature _____

THE LEGENDARY LOTTO TICKET-TO-WIN

☑ Yes, enter my ticket-to-win!

Sales Rep's Name ☐ DEMO

_____ ☐ SALE

Co. Name of Sale/Demo _____

Address _____

_____

Model # _____

Date of Sale/Demo _____

Branch Mgr./Dealer Owner Signature _____

THE LEGENDARY LOTTO TICKET-TO-WIN

☑ Yes, enter my ticket-to-win!

Sales Rep's Name ☐ DEMO

_____ ☐ SALE

Co. Name of Sale/Demo _____

Address _____

_____

Model # _____

Date of Sale/Demo _____

Branch Mgr./Dealer Owner Signature _____

Company Logo

THE LEGENDARY LOTTO

— RULES —

1. The program runs from July 1, 19___ to August 31, 19___.
2. For each product *demonstration* of products x, y and z, Sales Reps may fill out *one* "ticket-to-win".
3. For each product *sale* made of products x, y and z, Sales Reps may fill out *three* "tickets-to-win".
4. Fax in all your "tickets" to the Marketing Coordinator at Head Office by 4 p.m., Eastern Standard Time.
5. At 5 p.m., E.S.T., a weekly winner will be chosen by drawing a name from the hat of completed "tickets-to-win". Dealer Reps will be asked to provide a copy of the customer invoice as verification of a sale.
6. All tickets will accumulate over the term of the contest thereby increasing your chances to win more than once.
7. The weekly winning ticket will not be thrown back into the barrel.
8. The weekly winners are to choose their prizes from those featured on the program poster.
9. The top Sales Manager for each month of the program period may choose any two of the exciting prizes featured on the program poster. The top Sales Manager will be the one with the highest number of tickets submitted per Sales Representative.
10. The Branch Manager/Dealer Owner with the highest number of tickets per representative for the two month period may take a spouse/companion on a "Mad Weekend-for-two". You make your way to the hotel and we'll pay the rest.

    The top Branch Manager/Dealer Owner must be at 100% of his/her sales forecast in order to qualify.
11. Please allow 3-4 weeks for delivery of the prize merchandise.
12. In order to claim their merchandise, all program winners must be employees of the company or of its authorized Dealers at the end of the program period.

Company Logo

THE LATEST!
THE GREATEST!
CAR RALLY!

- ☑ Put Your Pedal to the Medal
- ☑ Achieve Top Sales Performance
- ☑ Join Us at the Annual Convention
- ☑ You Could Win A Brand New Car!

Company Logo

THE LATEST! THE GREATEST! CAR RALLY

DESCRIPTION   Your Field force will be charged into motion when they hear that they can win a brand new car!

Use this program as a build-up to your National Convention, if you have one.

PARTICIPANTS   Branch Managers, Dealer Owners, Sales Managers, Service Technicians, Branch Administrators, Sales Reps.

OTHER APPLICATIONS   Program can be modified to suit Government employees as well as manufacturing. Productivity/cost reduction could be the goal.

OBJECTIVES   1) Awesome team building program. Everybody helps each other to win.

2) Increase sales, reduce receivables, improve technical service to customers.

LENGTH   3 months - the last 3 months of the fiscal year.

DETAILS   The measurement levels and chequered flag prizes appear on the following pages. The monthly prizes are good; however, it's the thought of driving away from Convention in a brand new car that drives (no pun intended!) your people to perform their personal best.

Consider offering the winner a choice between a car or cash. Younger winners might choose the car, whereas older winners might prefer cold hard cash. A jeep could be a substitute for a car.

All tickets are brought to Convention and put into a large drum on the first day. Make a big deal of putting the tickets in the drum. Call out the names of the attendees and indicate how many tickets they have earned.

Winners must be present at Convention in order to receive their prize. Build excitement by conducting the draw on the last day of Convention. Picture, if you will, this excited winner running up to the podium to receive the keys to his/her brand new car. The applause will be deafening and you can believe that every

single person in that room will work harder next year in anticipation of being the big winner.

During the three month contest, hype the program 'til there's
no tomorrow. You can start with teaser mailings. ''Will you
be the next winner of a brand new car?'' That's all you need
is a one liner on company letterhead.

Follow up the teasers with the kick-off package. Include
brochures of the car that they can win. Send the package to
their home - the power of the spouse to motivate cannot be
over emphasized. Send a poster of the car to the Branch/Dealer
offices. Keep sending visual reminders of that end goal.

MEASUREMENT Determine what effect the program had on the YTD sales forecast, your receivables and service response times, etc.

Analyze the participation level within each category.

Analyze the total cost of the program as a % of sales.

Recommend changes, if any, for next year.

RECOGNITION At the end of each month, recognize the winners of the smaller
prizes. Ensure that the Branch Managers and Dealer Owners
have a special recognition ceremony for the monthly winners.

The National Sales Managers and President/CEO should send
a recognition letter to all the winners.

The greatest recognition for all the participants will come at
Convention when you call out the number of tickets that each
participant has earned. Have the winner of the car step into
his/her brand new car amidst raucous applause. (I'm assum-
ing you'll have the car on the convention floor.)

THE LATEST! THE GREATEST! CAR RALLY

CATEGORY	HOW YOU CAN WIN THE RACE!	CHECKERED FLAG WINNERS' PRIZES		
		APRIL	MAY	JUNE
BRANCH MANAGER DEALER OWNERS	Achieve greatest % over forecast of overall sales (or you may choose to target specific areas of sales, ie hardware)	Compact Disc Player	Valet Carry-on	35mm Camera

PLUS
All Branch Managers and Dealer Owners will receive the following # of tickets per contest month towards THE DRAW!

10 tickets per % over 100% of sales forecast
20 tickets per % over 105% of sales forecast
30 tickets per % over 110% of sales forecast
50 tickets per % over 115% of sales forecast

SALES MANAGER	Achieve greatest % over sales forecast	Car Stereo	35mm Camera	Micro-wave

PLUS
TOP Sales Manager for the quarter attends convention with 150 free tickets towards THE DRAW!

SERVICE TECHNICIAN	Highest achiever with fewest call backs, best response times, # of calls in a day, sale of service agreements and supplies.	Car Stereo	35mm Camera	Micro-wave

PLUS
TOP Technician for the quarter attends convention with 150 free tickets towards THE DRAW!

CATEGORY	HOW YOU CAN WIN THE RACE!	CHECKERED FLAG WINNERS' PRIZES		
		APRIL	MAY	JUNE
BRANCH ADMINISTRATION	Achieve lowest % of past due accounts receivable as a % of total receivables. (They can also be measured in age of inventory, accuracy of inventory, order processing corrections and number of charge backs.)	Micro-wave	35mm Camera	Diamond Pendant

PLUS
Top Branch Administrator
for the quarter attends
convention with 150
free tickets towards
THE DRAW!

CATEGORY	HOW YOU CAN WIN THE RACE!	CHECKERED FLAG WINNERS' PRIZES
SALES REPS	(Measure Sales Reps. accorded to a weighted program. See rules 1 & 2 of "U-TOP-IA".)	The winner in each month will receive a personally engraved leather briefcase. There are usually more people in the Sales Rep. category than in any other; therefore, it is advisable to have 2nd and 3rd prizes.

PLUS
TOP Sales Rep. *in each month* attends convention
with 150 free tickets towards
THE DRAW!

THE WINNER OF THE BRAND NEW CAR MUST BE PRESENT AT CONVENTION

Company Logo

HOW CAN YOU IMPROVE YOUR CHANCES TO WIN A BRAND NEW CAR?

Read on:

- STRIVE FOR YOUR PERSONAL BEST
- INTRODUCE PROSPECTS TO NEW PRODUCTS
- INTRODUCE YOUR CURRENT CUSTOMER BASE TO OUR NEW PRODUCTS AND SUPPLIES
- SELL OUT USED INVENTORY TO LUKE-WARM PROSPECTS
- SELL SERVICE AGREEMENTS, SELL ACCESSORIES
- REDUCE RECEIVABLES
- SELL, SELL, SELL. . .

GOOD LUCK!

Company Logo

IT'S SHOW TIME!

Now Playing:
DOUBLE FEATURE

DOUBLE YOUR EARNINGS!
DOUBLE YOUR FUN!

- Win a trip to Hawaii faster than you could have dreamed . . .

- Become a ''100% Club'' member in a flash . . .

- Buy that new jacket you've always wanted . . .

Company Logo

DOUBLE YOUR EARNINGS
DOUBLE YOUR FUN!

DESCRIPTION   "Did someone say I could double my commission this month and double my chances to go to Hawaii? Allright!"

PARTICIPANTS   Field Sales Reps in Branch and Dealer offices.

OTHER APPLICATIONS: The program's objectives and rules can be modified to suit:

1) Government Employees, Administrators, Plant Workers, Telemarketing Reps and Customer Support Employees: reward the best ideas for improving productivity, reducing costs and/or increasing profits. Increase your telephone sales, reduce receivables, accelerate billings, reduce manufacturing waste.

2) Service Technicians: reward an increase in the number of calls they make in a day, improve the quality of service, increase the sale of service contracts and lower-priced products (supplies, accessories, etc.).

3) All Employees: create or maintain a happy working environment. Generate ideas for increasing productivity, reducing costs and/or increasing profits.

4) Managers: improve productivity or sales per employee, create comraderie (a team) through friendly competition between managers.

This program can be run locally, regionally or nationally.

OBJECTIVE   1) To move slow-moving products
2) To share ideas on *how to sell* slow-moving products.

LENGTH   One month.

DEALER   If you have implemented the programs "The 100% Club" and "Dream Trippers", "Double Your Earnings, Double Your Fun" is a natural mind jogger for long distance programs. The annual programs often need reinforcement throughout the year. As discussed in "Dream Trippers", you can recognize the progress of the field force with a monthly newsletter. In addition, you can send the field little reminder packages of fun: sand, shells, beach balls, etc.

Occasionally, though, it is a good idea to give the field a real boost by doubling the earning power of their sales. At the same time, you will be ridding your warehouse of slow-moving products.

In "Double Your Earnings", the troops are given double points for each product sold/rented under the rules of "The 100% Club". You can also double the dollar value of the products sold under the rules of "Dream Trippers"

A rep that is close to winning a trip to Hawaii or a quarterly certificate to "The 100% Club", will hustle his/her butt to increase sales. I've seen it work wonders.

Take a look at any other long-term programs that you've got on board. "Double Your Earnings" may give the field the extra boost they need.

If you have no other programs with which to form an extension, then consider double commission dollars for certain products sold.

MEASUREMENT Determine the increase in sales of slow-moving products. What has happened to your profits?

Determine participation level by Branch rep, and Dealer rep.

Recommend changes, if any, to future programs.

RECOGNITION At your weekly sales meetings, recognize the individuals for their successes. Have them share ideas on how to sell these slow-moving products. If a lesson in "how to demo" is required, have your top achiever strutt his/her stuff.

At the month's close, recognize all "Double Your Earnings" achievers locally and nationally. Use the company newsletter as the communications vehicle. (See "Star Reach - The Newsletter".) Have the National Sales Manager and President/CEO send a personal letter of recognition to each "Double Your Earnings" recipient.

"THE" OPEN

Join The Club!

- A hole-in-one, you say?
- A birdie or a bogie?
- Improve your score in this exciting new 9 hole course!

Company Logo

"THE" OPEN

DESCRIPTION   Golf, as a sport, is growing at 10-15% annually. The Japanese call the golf course "The Green Boardroom". Your sales people will thoroughly enjoy this fun, 9 "hole" golf game.

The "Open" is a personalized program in that you can name it after your company ie "the ABC Open". For non-golfers who win each "hole", offer non-golf related prizes. That way, everyone will want to get in on the action. You can run this low-budget program by keeping the smaller prizes under $20 each.

PARTICIPANTS   Sales Reps in Branch and Dealer offices.

OTHER APPLICATIONS: The program's objectives and rules can be modified to suit:

1) Government Employees, Administrators, Plant Workers, Telemarketing Reps and Customer Support Employees: reward the best ideas for improving productivity, reducing costs and/or increasing profits. Increase your telephone sales, reduce receivables, accelerate billings, reduce manufacturing waste.

2) Service Technicians: reward an increase in the number of calls they make in a day, improve the quality of service, increase the sale of service contracts and lower-priced products (supplies, accessories, etc.).

3) All Employees: create or maintain a happy working environment. Generate ideas for increasing productivity, reducing costs and/or increasing profits.

4) Managers: improve productivity or sales per employee, create comraderie (a team) through friendly competition between managers.

This program can be run locally, regionally or nationally.

OBJECTIVES   1) To increase the number of new sales calls and product demos per week.

2) To increase sales for the length of the course.

LENGTH   9 holes! (one hole per week). The best time to run this program is during the golf season although it can certainly liven up the dull winter months.

DETAILS The contest "Rules" appear on the following pages.

Branch Managers/Dealer Owners are to collect all the information from the Sales Reps and fax the "Results Forms" in to Head Office. The Managers/Owners are to keep the supporting documents in the event that they are required for verification purposes.

The contest kick-off can be comprised of:
(1) Posters announcing the program.
(2) Individual Score Cards for the reps to carry. They'll write in their details for transfer later to the "Contest Results Form".
(3) Golf tees with company logo.
(4) Golf balls with company logo.

The tees and balls can be distributed at the kick-off meeting. The balls can be used as daily prizes, if you wish to hand out daily prizes.

MEASUREMENT Determine what effect the program has had on the Y-T-D sales forecast. Compare sales for this period versus the same period last year.

Calculate the increase in new sales calls and product demonstrations.

Determine the participation level by Branch/Dealership.

Calculate the cost of the program as a % of sales.

Recommend changes, if any, to future programs.

RECOGNITION If possible, gather the troops mid-week to assess their progress. Maybe hand out golf balls to early achievers. Exchange ideas on how to improve their "score".

Each Branch/Dealership should meet on Monday mornings to recognize their Winner for hole #x. If he/she has made the big time - National Winner - recognize that individual at your mid-week meeting (results will be faxed out on Tuesdays). He/she will get to choose 2 prizes. Runner-up to the Branch/Dealership Winner may also win golf balls.

Remind the troops at each meeting of the vast selection of weekly prizes that they can win. Pump them up over the Grand Prizes.

Have the President/CEO and the National Sales Manager of the company send a Letter of Recognition to the Branch/Dealership and National winners.

"THE" OPEN

— RULES —

1. 9 holes of golf will be played. Each hole has a specific activity associated with it. For example, Hole #2 is related to the number of customer calls made. The more new calls a rep makes, the better the score.
2. The contest begins _____, 19 ____ and ends _____, 19____.
3. PRIZES
   - WEEKLY PRIZES
     a) *one prize* for the lowest score in *each* Branch and in *each* participating Dealership.
     b) *two prizes* for the golfer with the lowest score attained *nationally*.

     Prizes will be chosen by the winners from the attached list of exciting prizes.
   - GRAND PRIZES will be won at the end of the 9 holes:
     a) the grand prize for the lowest national score is a set of brand name golf clubs.
     b) The runners-up grand prizes for the next four lowest national scores are brand name golf bags.

     NOTE: Non-golfers will be able to substitute their grand prizes for sporting equipment of their choice. The value will be equivalent to that of the clubs or bags.
4. In the event of a tie:
   a) For sales related "holes", the rep with the highest dollar volume in sales will win the prize(s).
   b) For non-sales related "holes", both winners many choose prizes.
   c) For the grand prizes, the Sales Reps with the highest dollar volume during the last four weeks of the contest will win the prize.
5. National winners for each "hole" will be announced via fax to each branch and participating dealer on the Tuesday following the end of each week's golf game.
6. Score cards and copies of sales order forms of each rep are to be submitted to the Branch Manager/Dealer Owner by the end of the contest week (8 p.m. Friday).

Continued. . .

7. Branch Managers/Dealer Owners must fax in the "Contest Results Form" for receipt by Head Office no later than 4:30 p.m. E.S.T. on the Monday following the last golf game.

8. Contest Results Forms received later than 4:30 p.m. on the Monday, will result in a penalty of 2 strokes for each rep listed on the form.

9. Non-reporting reps for a week will be given the highest score plus a penalty of 1 stroke. Two weeks of non-reporting will indicate that a rep or dealership has chosen not to participate.

10. New reps starting in the middle of the competition will be given points to get started. For example, if a new rep starts in the 5th week of the competition, he/she will receive the highest scores for holes 1-4 and will then begin competing on the 5th hole.

11. Winners of the grand prizes must be employees of either the company or an authorized dealership on the final day of Hole #9 in order to claim their prizes.

Company Logo

"THE" OPEN

HOLES 1 and 6		PAR 4		WEEKS OF (dates)
Score	**Activity**			
(8)	Quadruple Bogie	for	1	product demonstration
(7)	Triple Bogie	for	2	product demonstrations
(6)	Double Bogie	for	3	product demonstrations
(5)	Bogie	for	5	product demonstrations
(4)	Par	for	7	product demonstrations
(3)	Birdie	for	8	product demonstrations
(2)	Eagle	for	9	product demonstrations
(1)	Hole-In-One	for	11	product demonstrations

TO WIN! Send in demo reports and "Contest Results Form".

HOLES 2 and 8		PAR 3	WEEKS OF (dates)
Score	**Activity**		
(6)	Triple Bogie	- Less than 15 new sales calls	
(5)	Double Bogie	- 18 new sales calls	
(4)	Bogie	- 36 new sales calls	
(3)	Par	- 55 new sales calls	
(2)	Birdie	- 70 new sales calls	
(1)	Hole-In-One	- 90 new sales calls	

TO WIN! Send in your call reports and "Contest Results Form".

HOLE 3		PAR 5	WEEK OF (dates)
Score	**Activity**		
(8)	Quadruple Bogie	for	sale of 1 unit
(7)	Double Bogie	for	sales of 2 units
(6)	Bogie	for	sales of 3 units
(5)	Par	for	sales of 4 units
(4)	Birdie	for	sales of 5 units
(3)	Eagle	for	sales of 6 units
(2)	Double Eagle	for	sales of 7 units
(1)	Hole-In-One	for	sales of 8 units

TO WIN! Send in copies of sales order forms and "Contest Results Form".

HOLES 4 and 7   PAR 4   WEEKS OF (dates)

Score Activity

(7)	Quadruple Bogie	for 10 new calls and 2 product demonstrations
(6)	Double Bogie	for 20 new calls and 3 product demonstrations
(5)	Bogie	for 30 new calls and 4 product demonstrations
(4)	Par	for 50 new calls and 6 product demonstrations
(3)	Birdie	for 60 new calls and 8 product demonstrations
(2)	Eagle	for 70 new calls and 10 product demonstrations
(1)	Hole-In-One	80 + new calls and 12 product demonstrations

Note: If a player scores 30 new calls and 2 demos versus 4 demos, he/she will receive a score of (7). The score allocated is the one given to the activity of the same amount of demos.

HOLE 5   PAR 3   WEEKS OF (dates)

Score Activity

(6)	Quadruple Bogie	for less than $3,000 sales dollar volume
(5)	Double Bogie	for $4,000 sales dollar volume
(4)	Bogie	for $8,000 sales dollar volume
(3)	Par	for $16,000 sales dollar volume
(2)	Birdie	for $32,000 sales dollar volume
(1)	Hole-In-One	for $50,000 sales dollar volume

TO WIN! Send in copies of sales order forms and ''Contest Results Form''.

HOLE 9   PAR 3   WEEK OF (dates)

Score Activity

(6)	Quadruple Bogie	for less than $3,000 sales dollar volume for the last 4 weeks
(5)	Double Bogie	for $4,000 sales dollar volume for the last 4 weeks
(4)	Bogie	for $8,000 sales dollar volume for the last 4 weeks
(3)	Par	for $16,000 sales dollar volume for the last 4 weeks
(2)	Birdie	for $32,000 sales dollar volume for the last 4 weeks
(1)	Hole-In-One	for $50,000 sales dollar volume for the last 4 weeks

TO WIN! Send in copies of sales orders and ''Contest Results Form''.

Company Logo

"THE" OPEN

— CONTEST RESULTS FORM —

Branch/Dealership _____

WEEK OF _____ HOLE # _____

SALES REP	1 **# OF NEW CALLS/WEEK**	2 **# OF DEMOS/WEEK**	3 **# OF UNIT SALES**	4 **SALES DOLLAR VOLUME**

* COLUMN #4 MUST BE FILLED IN EACH WEEK IN CASE OF A TIE.

Please fill out this form each week, and send only the completed form to the Marketing Coordinator.
Hole # 1 & 6 — Fill in columns 2 & 4
Hole # 2 & 8 — Fill in columns 1 & 4
Hole # 3   — Fill in columns 3 & 4
Hole # 4 & 7 — Fill in columns 1, 2 & 4
Hole # 5 & 9 — Fill in column 4

*Proof of sales in the form of sales orders, call reports and product demonstration forms must be available upon request.

District Manager's/Dealer Owner's Signature _____

WEEKLY PRIZE LIST

CONGRATULATIONS! You have just earned the right to select from this list of great prizes.

GOLF RELATED PRIZES
Golf Hat
Putters
Golf Umbrella (assorted colours)
Knitted Head Club Covers
Golf Towels
10 in 1 Golf Tool
Electric Ball Returns
Brand Name Golf Glove
Beverage Cooler
Brand Name Shirts (assorted colours)
Brand Name Ball Retrievers
Golf Gloves & Golf Sock Gift Set

NON-GOLF RELATED PRIZES
1 Dozen Brand Name Tennis Balls
Cassette Cases
Badminton Set
Sports Socks
Solid Brass Picture Frames
Desk-Top Brass Business Card Holders
  (3 initials)
Brand Name Racquet Ball Racquet in
  Case
Sports Shorts
Brass Candlesticks
Clock Radios
Sports Glove
Hockey Bags
Lawn Darts
Sports Bags
Safety Glasses
Horseshoes
Figure Trimmer
Paddleball Set
Croquet Set

* NATIONAL WINNER - CHOOSE 2 PRIZES
* BRANCH WINNER - CHOOSE 1 PRIZE

Call your Marketing Coordinator at (   )   -   with your choice(s)

Company Logo

PART E:

A POTPOURRI OF 30 MORE IDEAS FOR INCENTIVE PROGRAMS

A POTPOURRI OF 30 MORE IDEAS FOR INCENTIVE PROGRAMS

Parts C and D of this book were filled with strong inspirational programs. Of course, there are dozens more ideas that come to mind. To produce them in detail would take a book of encyclopedic proportions! I've listed some of them here for you as a potpourri of ideas. Take the basic idea and turn it into a program or call me and I'll assist you. Once again, these are written, for the most part, for sales people. Modify them to suit any category of employee or dealer.

THE POTPOURRI

1. **"TOUCHDOWN!"** - Design this program around a football theme. Launch it with hot chocolate, a helmet worn by the Manager, music of football fight songs, tickets to local football games, etc. Per sale of a product, the participant can enter a ticket to win. Prizes: TV's, stereos, disc players, weekly draws.

2. **"CASH 'N CARRY"** - Offer cash as a reward for selling complete packages of products. This will encourage Sales Reps to sell hardware, service and supplies as a complete package.

3. **"PRESIDENT'S DAY PROMO"** - Same design as "National Demothon Days" with a couple exceptions. Your Dealers can receive better pricing on certain products. Their reps and Sales Manager will receive cash (bearing the faces of various Presidents) for products sold.

4. **"COMPLETE THE SALES PICTURE"** - For every unit sold, the Sales Rep receives another piece of a jigsaw puzzle. When the puzzle is complete, it forms the picture of a video camera which he/she wins.

5. **"POT OF GOLD AT THE END OF THE RAINBOW"** - Each salesperson has a rainbow next to his/her name on a wall chart. Every time a sale is made, the pot of gold moves along the rainbow. The first person to reach the end of the rainbow wins a pot of gold!

6. **"NATIONAL DEMO COMPETITION"** - A marvellous recognition vehicle. Have local reps compete to choose the rep with the best product demonstration skills. They will advance to a regional competition and then to a national competition. The two best reps will be the stars in a video tape which can be used as a training tool for everyone.

7. **"DEAR SPOUSE"** - A great way to involve the spouse at home. Send a letter to him/her indicating that they can win a large screen TV if the spouse makes sales quota. The spouse at home can even pick out the model.

8. **"WIN YOUR WAY TO THE SUPERBOWL"** - The top 5 sales reps win their way to the Superbowl. Throw in a category for top Branch Manager, Regional Manager, Dealer Owner. Use terms like Leading Scorer, Leading Passer, Leading Rusher.

9. **"LET'S PLAY POKER"** - For every unit of sales, the salesperson gets a playing card. The rep with the most cards has the best chance of making the winning poker hand. The next best hand and third best hands can also win. Prizes could include portable pool tables and wooden chess sets.

10. **"LEAD ME TO THE CHURCH ON TIME"** - You've heard the expression "one for the church" or one for the corporate coffers? Design a sales lead program where all employees can get involved. For every lead generated for the "church", $x is thrown into a pot. At the end of the contest period, the employee with the most leads which result in a sale will win a portion of the pot. There should be 2nd and 3rd prizes like barbecues and T-bone steaks. Since sales people have more access to leads, "weight" all the employees to give everyone a fair chance or eliminate Sales people from this contest.

11. **"SHOPPING SPREE"**- The top sales people or top employees with the best program for profits win a shopping spree. Another great program to send to the home - get the spouse involved. Some of your best ideas will probably come from the spouses.

12. **"WHEEL OF FORTUNE"** - If you have lots of money, you can rent a wheel for each branch. A more simple method is to have one wheel reside at Head Office and a chosen employee (someone who deserves recognition) will spin the wheel for the Sales Rep with the most sales or demos for the week. Valuable prizes are on the wheel. Send each Rep a paper wheel showing the prizes they can win.

13. **"CHRISTMAS STOCKING"** - Each Sales Rep receives a red stocking with a beautiful piece of silver flatware in it. The note attached says. ''To get the rest, all you have to do is this ... .''

14. **"INITIALLY YOURS"** - For top employees with the best ideas, best sales, most leads etc., allow them to choose a prize that starts with the same initial as their name. Example: Diana may choose a Diamond Ring of a value up to $x.

15 **"LIFESTYLES OF THE RICH AND SUCCESSFUL"** - Top employees win getaway vacations to luxury spots. It could be a local resort or a tropical island whichever your budget can afford.

16. **"THINK BIG"** - Send out buttons, keychains, coasters, etc. with this message printed on them. Top achievers win something big like a windsurfer, rowing machine or racing bike.

17. **"REACH FOR THE STARS"** - For every sale, the rep receives huge silver or gold stars. Make a list of prizes that they can win. As the value of the prize escalates, the more stars are required to win. At the end of the contest period (try 2-3 months), everyone can cash in their stars and choose a prize. Another good one to send to the home.

18. **"PRODUCT REFUND"** - A great way to get your Sales Reps using your own products at home. Say, you're a computer company. Memo-bill the rep and refund him $x as per his/her sales performance up to the value of the computer.

19. **"STOCK STAMPEDE"** - Top achievers win shares of stock.

20. **"FERRARI FEVER"** - Top achievers win the use of a top sports car for a year.

21. **"FUR FANTASY"** - Top achievers win a fur jacket of their choice up to value x for him/her and spouse. Send info to the home.

22. **"THE EIGHTH WONDER OF THE WORLD"** - Top Sales Rep of the year (the eighth wonder) wins a trip for two to visit a few of the original seven wonders of the world.

23. ***"MONEY GROWS ON TREES"*** - Send each sales rep a paper tree with their name on it. The tree has spots to which phoney money can be attached. For each sale or demo, the Branch Manager recognizes the employee by handing him a phoney $10 bill. Once the tree is filled, the Sales Rep wins real money by cashing in his phoney bills.

24. ***"KICK OFF KIBITZER"*** - Introduce a new product. The first Sales Rep to sell x number of products in 4 days wins a prize - new leather shoes or boots.

25. ***"CHIPPER CRAZY"*** - For every sale or demo, hand out poker chips. Each Rep can receive a velvet bag with Las Vegas stamped on it in which to keep their chips. At the end of the contest period, the Rep with the most chips wins a trip to Vegas. Offer second and third prizes.

26. ***"STAMP STAMINA"*** - Send each Sales Rep a promo sheet divided into squares upon which they can place stamps. The stamps can be imprinted with various prizes. After each sale, he/she can stick their own stamp to the promo sheet. Once the sheet is full, they get to choose any prize imprinted on the stamps.

27. ***"BE A HERO"*** - Top dealer of the year receives $3,000 from you to donate to a local charity. Arrange press coverage. Honor the hero.

28. ***"KNOWLEDGE PAYS"*** - A great program for high tech products. Each Sales Rep and/or Service Tech receives a product manual. A quiz is later sent to test their knowledge - your choice of open or closed book. Top scorer receives a prize. Offer secondary prizes.

29. ***"WARDROBE SIZZLER"*** - Top Dealer, Top Employee or Top Sales Rep could win a brand new wardrobe. Manager joins them on a shopping spree and takes the winner and a guest out for dinner.

30. ***"WRITE FOR WINNINGS"*** - Three top written sales presentations win 35 mm cameras. The top of the three gets an extra zoom lens.

CLOSING WORD

Publishing this book has been a major highlight in my life. My goal was to communicate to you the kind of knowledge that comes from day to day experience. Let me know about the programs you've implemented. If I can be of any assistance to you in developing future programs, feel free to write or fax.

Studies of the best organizations have shown that they have the following characteristics:
- clear goals
- teamwork - everyone is important, equal participation
- freedom to try ideas
- short and long term rewards
- follow-up/implementation plans
- open communications
- esprit de corps
- talented people
- delegation of responsibility and authority
- discipline
- commitment to common goals
- high purpose
- high positive energies - happy employees
- continually learning

As you put together your plans with which to Create Champions, remember this:

WHEN YOUR STAFF SUCCEEDS, SO DO YOU.

BIBLIOGRAPHY

Blanchard, Kenneth and Spencer Johnson *The One Minute Manager*. New York: William Morrow and Company, Inc. 1982.

Gerber, Michael E. *The E Myth*. New York: Harper Business, 1986.

LeBoeuf, Michael, *The Greatest Management Principle* in the World. New York: Berkley, 1986.

McKay, Edward S., *The Marketing Mystique*. New York: Amacom, 1979.

Naisbitt, John, *Megatrends*. New York: Warner Books Inc., 1984.

Peters, Thomas J. and Nancy K. Austin, *A Passion For Excellence*. New York: Random House, 1985.

Peters, Thomas J. and Robert H. Waterman, *In Search of Excellence*. New York: Harper & Row, 1982.

Rapp, Stan and Tom Collins, *Maxi-Marketing*. New York: McGraw-Hill, 1988.

Ziglar, Zig, *Top Performance*. New York: Berkley, 1987.

INDEX

ABOUT THE AUTHOR

B. K-BURR
AUTHOR, MOTIVATIONAL SPEAKER, TRAINER, CONSULTANT

B. K-Burr has had a varied and wonderful career as a diplomat, as a sales and marketing executive and now as an author, motivational speaker, trainer and consultant.

Listed below are highlights from the author's career:

- 6 years as a Diplomat serving in Paris, France, London, England, Berne, Switzerland and Ottawa, Canada.

- With countless number of years of experience in large international corporations, start-up companies and government, B. K-Burr has a broad background in both the private and public sectors.

- The author has held management positions in such "excellent" companies as 3M and Lanier, two of "America's best-run companies." *

- B. K-Burr is renowned for developing expert motivation programs for employees at all levels of the organization.

- As a specialist in understanding how and why the customer buys, the author has created English and French sales tools adopted by company subsidiaries world-wide.

B. K-Burr is the President of K-Burr and Associates, a company specializing in management training, consulting, the development of motivational programs and the creation of sales tools which truly help sell product.

* Peters, Thomas J. and Robert H. Waterman, *In Search of Excellence*. New York: Harper & Row, 1982.

HELP LINE

HELP IS BUT A FAX CALL AWAY. FAX OR MAIL IN THIS PAGE TO THE ADDRESS GIVEN. THE AUTHOR WILL CONTACT YOU AS SOON AS POSSIBLE.

Yes, I have read *Creating Champions* and I need help. (PLEASE CHECK ☑)

☐ I think my employees are unhappy, help me motivate them.

☐ I need help motivating my Dealers.

☐ I need help setting goals.

☐ Teamwork is lacking.

☐ Train me to be a better Leader.

☐ Help me set up a Recognition and Praise program for all employees.

☐ Help me design sales incentive programs for my sales force.

☐ We need a better customer service program.

☐ My sales force needs better sales tools.

☐ Help me to excecute the incentive programs in your book.

☐ I need help selling the ideas in this book to my boss.

☐ Other, please describe _____

_____

_____

MY NAME IS _____

MY TITLE IS _____

NAME OF ORGANIZATION _____

STREET_____ CITY_____

STATE/PROVINCE _____ ZIP/P.C. _____

MY BUSINESS PHONE # _____ MY FAX # _____

DESCRIBE YOUR PRODUCTS/SERVICES _____

_____

_____

MAIL TO: K-BURR & ASSOCIATES
P.O. BOX 21024
LONDON, ONTARIO N6J 1G0
CANADA   OR   FAX (519) 649-4509

ORDER FORM
TRAINING PROGRAMS AND LEARNING TOOLS

K-Burr & Associates is a group of highly experienced professionals whose prime purpose is to train and consult in the public and private sectors. We focus on leadership training, team-building, customer service and balancing career and personal lives.

Yes, I am interested in the following programs and learning tools:
(PLEASE CHECK ☑)

TRAINING PROGRAMS

☐ Creating Champions — Making the Leap from Manager to Coach and Leader
☐ Teambuilding
☐ Customer Service
☐ Managing Your Life! Balancing Career and Home.

LEARNING TOOLS

☐ MORE COPIES OF *CREATING CHAMPIONS*
☐ PERSONAL PROFILE SYSTEM (DISC)   @ $19.95
☐ TIME MANAGEMENT PROFILE   @ $19.95
☐ CUSTOMER SERVICE PROFILE   @ $19.95
☐ COUPLE'S PROFILE   @ $24.95

MY NAME IS _____
MY TITLE IS _____
NAME OF ORGANIZATION _____
STREET _____ CITY _____
STATE/PROVINCE _____ ZIP/P.C. _____
MY BUSINESS PHONE # _____ MY FAX # _____
DESCRIBE YOUR PRODUCTS/SERVICES _____
_____
_____

MAIL TO: K-BURR & ASSOCIATES
         P.O. BOX 21024
         LONDON, ONTARIO N6J 1G0
         CANADA
  OR   FAX (519) 649-4509

ORDER FORM - GRAPHICS

To help me *save thousands of dollars* on new artwork, please send me an 8 1/2'' x 11'' coated paper copy (ready for imprinting with my logo) of the original artwork for each of the following incentive programs: (PLEASE CHECK ☑)

- ☐ The 100% Club.
- ☐ Dream Trippers.
- ☐ Star Reach - A Dealer Program.
- ☐ Star Reach - The Newsletter.
- ☐ Spring Wings.
- ☐ Kookie Kapers.
- ☐ U-TOP-IA!
- ☐ The Royal Marketing Academy.
- ☐ The Steeplechase.
- ☐ Santa's Christmas Bag.
- ☐ National Demothon Days.
- ☐ Auction Bucks.
- ☐ The Pro Golf Celebrity Classic.
- ☐ Undercover Agent.
- ☐ The Legendary Lotto.
- ☐ The Latest! The Greatest! Car Rally.
- ☐ Double Your Earnings! Double Your Fun!
- ☐ ''The'' Open.

TOTAL # OF PROGRAMS ORDERED   =   _____

X $45 U.S. ($55 CDN. including taxes) = $_____ enclosed.

MY NAME IS _____

MY TITLE IS _____

NAME OF ORGANIZATION _____

STREET _____ CITY _____

STATE/PROVINCE _____ ZIP/P.C. _____

MY BUSINESS PHONE # _____ MY FAX # _____

DESCRIBE YOUR PRODUCTS/SERVICES _____

_____

_____

MAIL TO: K-BURR & ASSOCIATES
        P.O. BOX 21024
        LONDON, ONTARIO N6J 1G0   FAX (519) 649-4509